# Cooking Light.

# MICROWAVE

# Cooking Light®

## MICROWAVE

### 80 Nutritious and Tempting Recipes for Soups, Salads, Main Courses, Desserts, and Beverages

**WARNER BOOKS**

A Time Warner Company

PHOTOGRAPHER: *Jim Bathie*

PHOTO STYLIST: *Kay E. Clarke*

BOOK DESIGN: *Giorgetta Bell McRee*

COVER DESIGN: *Andrew Newman*

---

Warner Books, Inc., 666 Fifth Avenue, New York, NY 10103

 A Time Warner Company

Printed in the United States of America
First printing: February 1991
10  9  8  7  6  5  4  3  2  1

**Library of Congress Cataloging-in-Publication Data**

Cooking light microwave / [photographer: Jim Bathie].
    p.    cm.—(Cooking light)
Includes index.
ISBN 0–446–39181–6
    1. Low-calorie diet—Recipes.   2. Low-fat diet—Recipes.
3. Microwave cookery.   I. Series: Cooking light (New York, N.Y.)
RM222.2.C599   1989
641.5′635—dc20                   90–44006
                                      CIP

# CONTENTS

EATING WELL IS THE BEST REWARD   *vii*

EDITOR'S NOTE   *ix*

SOUPS   *1*

SALADS AND DRESSINGS   *4*

MAIN DISHES   *15*

RICE AND COUSCOUS   *40*

VEGETABLES   *45*

CONDIMENTS   *53*

DESSERTS   *55*

BEVERAGES   *72*

INDEX   *75*

# EATING WELL IS THE BEST REWARD

Welcome to **Cooking Light,** a cookbook that celebrates the pleasures of good health. These low-fat, low-calorie recipes are easy to make, a delight to behold, and a feast for the senses.

Guided by the belief that good health and good food are synonymous, **Cooking Light** provides an approach to eating and cooking that is both healthy and appealing. Using the eighty recipes in this book, you will see how easy it is to minimize fat and sodium while maximizing minerals, fiber, and vitamins. And you will be delighted by the emphasis on the good taste and texture of fresh wholesome food cooked the light way.

So eat hearty, slim down and delight yourself, your family, and your friends with these easy-to-prepare, all-natural, and very delicious recipes.

# EDITOR'S NOTE

*Unless otherwise indicated:*

eggs are large

margarine is corn oil margarine

sugar is granulated white sugar

flour is all-purpose

two knives can be used instead of a pastry blender

raisins are "dark"

muffin pans are 2½ inches

cranberries and other ingredients are fresh

prepared mustard is regular store-bought yellow mustard

all noodles are cooked without fat or salt

Dutch process cocoa is alkalized

chicken breast is cooked without skin and without salt

vinegar is regular distilled vinegar

# Cooking Light®

## MICROWAVE

# SOUPS

---

## HERBED TOMATO BOUILLON

---

1 teaspoon beef-flavored bouillon granules
1 cup hot water
3 cups no-salt-added tomato juice
2 tablespoons chopped fresh parsley
1 tablespoon lemon juice
1 teaspoon low-sodium Worcestershire sauce
½ teaspoon dried whole rosemary
¼ teaspoon dried whole thyme
¼ teaspoon pepper
Lemon slices (optional)

Dissolve bouillon granules in hot water; add tomato juice and next 6 ingredients, stirring well. Cover with heavy-duty plastic wrap, and microwave at HIGH for 3 to 5 minutes or until bouillon mixture is hot. To serve, ladle bouillon into soup bowls. Garnish each serving with a lemon slice, if desired. Yield: 4 cups (43 calories per 1 cup serving).

PROTEIN 1.9 / FAT 0.3 / CARBOHYDRATE 10.1 / CHOLESTEROL 0 / IRON 0.3 / SODIUM 262 / CALCIUM 7

# CREAMY GREEN CHILE SOUP

1 cup chopped onion
1 cup chopped celery
2 cloves garlic, minced
1 tablespoon reduced-calorie margarine
3 tablespoons all-purpose flour
1 teaspoon chicken-flavored bouillon granules
2 cups hot water
2 cups skim milk
¼ teaspoon chili powder
⅛ teaspoon ground red pepper
2 (4-ounce) cans chopped green chiles, drained
¼ cup plus 2 tablespoons (1½ ounces) shredded 40%
   less-fat Cheddar cheese

Combine onion, celery, garlic, and margarine in a 3-quart casserole. Cover with heavy-duty plastic wrap, and microwave at HIGH for 3 to 4 minutes or until crisp-tender. Add flour; stir well. Dissolve bouillon granules in hot water. Gradually add bouillon, milk, chili powder, and pepper to mixture, stirring well. Microwave at HIGH for 8 to 10 minutes or until slightly thickened, stirring every 3 minutes. Stir in chiles, and microwave at HIGH for 1 minute. Stir well before serving. To serve, ladle soup into individual serving bowls. Top each serving with 1 tablespoon cheese. Serve immediately. Yield: 6 cups (94 calories per 1-cup serving).

PROTEIN 5.1 / FAT 2.7 / CARBOHYDRATE 12.9 / CHOLESTEROL 2 / IRON 0.4 / SODIUM 282 / CALCIUM 166

# QUICK VEGETABLE-BEEF SOUP

½ pound ground chuck
¼ cup chopped green pepper
¼ cup chopped onion
1 (14½-ounce) can stewed tomatoes, undrained
1 cup frozen mixed vegetables
1 cup water
¼ teaspoon dried whole basil
⅛ teaspoon garlic powder
½ teaspoon freshly ground pepper

Combine ground chuck, green pepper, and onion in a 2-quart casserole; cover with heavy-duty plastic wrap, and microwave at HIGH for 4 minutes or until meat is no longer pink, stirring after 2 minutes. Drain well in a colander, and pat dry with paper towels. Wipe casserole dry with a paper towel. Return drained meat mixture to casserole.

Add remaining ingredients to meat mixture. Cover and microwave at HIGH for 9 to 10 minutes, stirring every 3 minutes. Ladle into individual serving bowls; serve hot. Yield: 4 cups (163 calories per 1-cup serving).

PROTEIN 14.4 / FAT 5.3 / CARBOHYDRATE 14.3 / FIBER 1.2 / CHOLESTEROL 40 / SODIUM 304 / POTASSIUM 551

# SALADS AND DRESSINGS

## ASPARAGUS SALAD WITH WATERCRESS DRESSING

1½ pounds fresh asparagus spears
¼ cup water
6 Bibb lettuce leaves
Watercress Dressing (recipe follows)
1 (4-ounce) jar chopped pimiento, drained

Snap off tough ends of asparagus. Remove scales from spears with a knife or vegetable peeler, if desired. Cut asparagus into 1½-inch pieces. Place in an 11- x 7- x 2-inch baking dish; add the water. Cover with heavy-duty plastic wrap, and microwave at HIGH for 6 to 7 minutes or until crisp-tender; drain. Cover and chill.

Spoon ½ cup chilled asparagus onto each of 6 lettuce-lined salad plates. Spoon 2 tablespoons Watercress Dressing over each salad, reserving remaining dressing for other uses. Top each salad evenly with chopped pimiento. Yield: 6 servings (33 calories per serving).

### Watercress Dressing:

½ cup plain nonfat yogurt
½ cup torn watercress
2 green onions, sliced
1 tablespoon chopped fresh parsley

1 tablespoon lemon juice
2 teaspoons Dijon mustard
¼ teaspoon salt
¼ teaspoon dried whole tarragon
⅛ teaspoon pepper

Combine all ingredients in container of an electric blender; process until smooth. Cover and chill. Yield: 1 cup.

PROTEIN 3.4 / FAT 0.3 / CARBOHYDRATE 5.4 / CHOLESTEROL 0 / IRON 0.9 / SODIUM 128 / CALCIUM 56

# GREEN SALAD WITH WARM BRIE DRESSING

2 tablespoons coarsely chopped walnuts
1 ounce Brie cheese
1 cup torn Boston lettuce
1 cup torn romaine lettuce
⅓ cup reduced-calorie Italian dressing

Spread walnuts in a 6-ounce custard cup. Microwave at HIGH for 3 to 4 minutes or until walnuts are lightly toasted, stirring after every minute. Set aside.

Remove rind from brie; cut cheese into small pieces. Set aside. Place lettuces in a large bowl, tossing gently to combine. Arrange lettuce mixture evenly on individual salad plates. Set aside.

Place dressing in a 1-cup glass measure. Microwave, uncovered, at HIGH for 30 seconds or until thoroughly heated. Add Brie, stirring until cheese melts. To serve, spoon dressing evenly over each salad. Top each serving with 1½ teaspoons reserved chopped walnuts. Yield: 4 servings (60 calories per serving).

PROTEIN 2.8 / FAT 4.2 / CARBOHYDRATE 3.1 / CHOLESTEROL 7 / IRON 0.3 / SODIUM 227 / CALCIUM 21

# HOT THREE-BEAN SALAD

1 (10-ounce) package frozen baby lima beans
½ cup water
1 (10-ounce) package frozen cut green beans
1 (15-ounce) can kidney beans, drained and rinsed
1 (4-ounce) jar sliced pimiento, drained
1 small purple onion, thinly sliced
½ cup cider vinegar
1 tablespoon sugar
2¾ teaspoons vegetable oil
½ teaspoon celery seeds
½ teaspoon dry mustard
¼ teaspoon salt
¼ teaspoon ground red pepper
¼ teaspoon paprika

Place lima beans in a 2-quart casserole; add the water. Cover with wax paper, and microwave at HIGH for 10 minutes, stirring after 5 minutes. Add green beans; cover and microwave at HIGH for 6 minutes or until green beans are crisp-tender. Drain. Return beans to casserole; add kidney beans, pimiento, and onion, stirring gently to combine.

Combine vinegar and remaining ingredients in a jar. Cover tightly and shake vigorously. Pour dressing mixture over vegetable mixture, stirring gently to combine. Cover and let stand at room temperature 30 minutes. Microwave at HIGH for 4 to 5 minutes or until thoroughly heated, stirring once. Serve warm. Yield: 8 servings (125 calories per ¾-cup serving).

PROTEIN 6.3 / FAT 2.0 / CARBOHYDRATE 21.9 / CHOLESTEROL 0 / IRON 2.7 / SODIUM 134 / CALCIUM 44

# PINEAPPLE SALAD WITH POPPY SEED DRESSING

Curly leaf lettuce leaves
1 medium-size fresh pineapple
2 medium kiwis, peeled
Poppy Seed Dressing (recipe follows)

Place lettuce leaves on a serving platter; set aside.

Peel and trim eyes from pineapple, removing core. Cut pineapple crosswise into 6 slices. Arrange over lettuce leaves. Cut kiwis into 6 slices; arrange over pineapple slices. Pour 2 tablespoons Poppy Seed Dressing over each serving. Yield: 6 servings (111 calories per serving).

## Poppy Seed Dressing:

¾ cup unsweetened orange juice
2 teaspoons cornstarch
1 tablespoon honey
1½ teaspoons poppy seeds
¼ teaspoon grated orange rind

Combine orange juice and cornstarch in a 2-cup glass measure, stirring well. Microwave at HIGH for 2½ minutes or until thickened, stirring once. Add honey, poppy seeds, and orange rind; stir well. Cover and chill. Yield: ¾ cup.

PROTEIN 1.4 / FAT 1.1 / CARBOHYDRATE 26.2 / CHOLESTEROL 0 / IRON 0.8 / SODIUM 4 / CALCIUM 34

# SWEET PEPPER SALAD

2 medium-size green peppers, cut into julienne strips
1 medium-size sweet red pepper, cut into julienne strips
¼ cup thinly sliced green onions
2 tablespoons red wine vinegar
1 tablespoon olive oil
1 tablespoon water
1 small clove garlic, minced
1 teaspoon sugar
½ teaspoon dried Italian seasoning
⅛ teaspoon salt

Combine pepper strips in a large bowl; set aside. Combine green onions and remaining ingredients in a 1-cup glass measure; stir well. Microwave, uncovered, at HIGH for 1½ to 2½ minutes or until mixture boils. Pour over pepper strips. Cover and chill thoroughly. Yield: 4 servings (56 calories per ½-cup serving).

PROTEIN 0.8 / FAT 3.7 / CARBOHYDRATE 5.5 / CHOLESTEROL 0 / IRON 1.2 / SODIUM 76 / CALCIUM 15

# SPINACH SALAD WITH YOGURT–POPPY SEED DRESSING

1 medium orange
¼ pound spinach leaves, washed and trimmed
½ cup sliced water chestnuts
2 tablespoons thinly sliced green onions
Yogurt-Poppy Seed Dressing (recipe follows)

Grate ½ teaspoon orange rind; reserve for use in Yogurt-Poppy Seed Dressing. Peel, seed, and section orange.
    Place spinach leaves on a serving platter. Arrange orange sections in a circular pattern on spinach, overlapping sections.

Combine water chestnuts and green onions; place in center of salad. Top with dressing. Yield: 4 servings (90 calories per serving).

## Yogurt–Poppy Seed Dressing:

3 tablespoons plain low-fat yogurt
3 tablespoons reduced-calorie mayonnaise
2 teaspoons honey
½ teaspoon grated orange rind
1 teaspoon poppy seeds

Combine all ingredients; stir with a wire whisk until smooth. Cover; chill. Yield: ⅓ cup.

PROTEIN 2.2 / FAT 3.7 / CARBOHYDRATE 13.4 / CHOLESTEROL 4 / IRON 1.0 / SODIUM 116 / CALCIUM 76

# CHERRY TOMATO SALAD

⅓ pound cherry tomatoes, quartered
¼ pound yellow plum tomatoes, quartered
1 small purple onion, thinly sliced and halved
¼ cup plus 2 tablespoons reduced-calorie ranch-style dressing
½ small avocado, peeled, pitted, and diced

Arrange tomatoes and onion on a large serving platter. Drizzle dressing down center of salad. Top with diced avocado. Yield: 6 servings (76 calories per serving).

PROTEIN 1.0 / FAT 6.2 / CARBOHYDRATE 9.6 / CHOLESTEROL 0 / IRON 0.5 / SODIUM 130 / CALCIUM 13

# ASPARAGUS–YELLOW SQUASH SALAD

1 pound fresh asparagus spears, diagonally sliced
2 tablespoons water
1 pound yellow squash, sliced
3 tablespoons freshly squeezed lemon juice
1 tablespoon finely chopped green onions
2 teaspoons olive oil
2 teaspoons Dijon mustard
½ teaspoon dried whole basil
¼ teaspoon pepper

Combine asparagus and the water in a 2-quart casserole. Cover with heavy-duty plastic wrap and vent; microwave at HIGH 2 minutes. Add squash and microwave at HIGH 4 minutes or until vegetables are tender, stirring after 2 minutes. Let stand, covered, 2 minutes.

Combine lemon juice and remaining ingredients in a small bowl; stir until well blended. Pour lemon juice mixture over vegetables, and toss lightly to coat well. Cover and chill thoroughly. Stir well before serving. Yield: 4 servings (74 calories per serving).

PROTEIN 4.9 / FAT 2.9 / CARBOHYDRATE 10.4 / CHOLESTEROL 0 / IRON 1.4 / SODIUM 79 / CALCIUM 52

# SWEET POTATO SALAD

¾ **pound sweet potatoes, peeled and cubed**
**3 tablespoons water**
**1 tablespoon vegetable oil**
**1 tablespoon lemon juice**
½ **teaspoon sugar**
**Curly leaf lettuce leaves**

Place sweet potatoes and the water in a 1-quart casserole. Cover with lid, and microwave at HIGH for 6 to 7 minutes, stirring after 3 minutes. Let stand 2 minutes. Drain potatoes well, and set aside.

Combine vegetable oil, lemon juice, and sugar; pour over reserved potatoes. Toss gently to coat. Serve at room temperature on curly leaf lettuce leaves. Yield: 4 servings (122 calories per serving).

PROTEIN 1.4 / FAT 3.7 / CARBOHYDRATE 21.5 / CHOLESTEROL 0 / IRON 0.5 / SODIUM 11 / CALCIUM 19

# TOMATO-VEGETABLE ASPIC

2 cups tomato juice
2 sprigs fresh parsley
1 bay leaf
¼ teaspoon dried whole basil
1 envelope unflavored gelatin
¼ cup cold water
1 tablespoon lemon juice
2 to 3 drops hot sauce
¼ cup finely chopped cucumber
¼ cup finely chopped celery
¼ cup finely chopped sweet red pepper
1 tablespoon minced onion
Vegetable cooking spray
24 very thin slices cucumber

Combine first 4 ingredients in a 2-quart mixing bowl. Cover with heavy-duty plastic wrap and microwave at HIGH for 5 to 6 minutes or until boiling; stir well. Cover and microwave at HIGH an additional 2 minutes. Strain, discarding herbs.

Soften gelatin in the cold water 1 minute; add to hot tomato juice mixture, stirring until gelatin dissolves. Stir in lemon juice and hot sauce. Chill until the consistency of unbeaten egg white.

Stir in cucumber, celery, sweet red pepper, and onion. Pour into 4 (6-ounce) molds coated with cooking spray. Chill overnight. Arrange cucumber slices on individual plates. Unmold chilled aspic onto cucumber slices to serve. Yield: 4 servings (37 calories per serving).

PROTEIN 2.8 / FAT 0.2 / CARBOHYDRATE 7.5 / FIBER 1.1 / CHOLESTEROL 0 / SODIUM 452 / POTASSIUM 541

# WILTED LETTUCE SALAD

4 cups torn red leaf lettuce
4 cups torn iceberg lettuce
¾ cup sliced fresh mushrooms
¾ cup oil-free Italian salad dressing

Combine first 3 ingredients in a large salad bowl; toss lightly, and set aside.

Place dressing in a 2-cup glass measure. Cover with heavy-duty plastic wrap, and microwave at HIGH for 1 to 2 minutes or until mixture boils. Immediately pour over lettuce mixture, tossing until well coated. Serve immediately. Yield: 8 servings (38 calories per serving).

PROTEIN 0.8 / FAT 3.1 / CARBOHYDRATES 2.2 / FIBER 0.5 / CHOLESTEROL 12 / SODIUM 31 / POTASSIUM 87

# FRUIT SALAD WITH CITRUS DRESSING

1 (8-ounce) can unsweetened pineapple tidbits, undrained
1½ teaspoons cornstarch
¼ cup unsweetened orange juice
¼ teaspoon grated lemon rind
Dash of ground cinnamon
1 cup seedless red grapes, halved
1 medium banana, peeled and sliced
1 kiwi, peeled and sliced
1 teaspoon lemon juice
4 orange cups
Bibb lettuce leaves

Drain pineapple, reserving ¼ cup juice in a 2-cup glass measure. Set pineapple aside.

Add cornstarch to reserved juice, stirring until well blended. Stir in orange juice, lemon rind, and cinnamon. Microwave at HIGH for 1½ to 2 minutes or until mixture begins to boil; stir. Microwave at HIGH for an additional 30 seconds to 1 minute or until thickened. Cool; cover and chill thoroughly.

Combine reserved pineapple, grapes, banana, kiwi, and lemon juice in a medium bowl; toss gently. Spoon equal amounts of fruit into orange cups; place each cup on a lettuce leaf. Serve with 2 tablespoons dressing per serving. Yield: 4 servings (104 calories per serving).

PROTEIN 1.3 / FAT 0.6 / CARBOHYDRATES 25.7 / FIBER 2.5 / CHOLESTEROL 0 / SODIUM 4 / POTASSIUM 380

# MAIN DISHES

## CREOLE EGGS

¼ pound sliced fresh mushrooms
¼ cup chopped onion
¼ cup chopped green pepper
¼ cup water
2 (8-ounce) cans no-salt-added tomato sauce
¼ teaspoon salt
¼ teaspoon dried whole thyme
¼ teaspoon pepper
4 eggs
2 English muffins, split and toasted

Combine first 4 ingredients in a 10- x 6- x 2-inch baking dish; cover with heavy-duty plastic wrap, and microwave at HIGH for 3 to 4 minutes, stirring after 2 minutes. Drain well, and return to baking dish.

Combine tomato sauce, salt, thyme, and pepper in a small bowl; stir well, and add to sautéed vegetables. Cover with heavy-duty plastic wrap, and microwave at HIGH for 4 to 5 minutes or until mixture comes to a boil.

Break eggs, one at a time, into a 6-ounce custard cup. Gently slip each egg into sauce mixture, and pierce yolk with a wooden pick. Cover with heavy-duty plastic wrap, and microwave at MEDIUM-HIGH (70% power) for 5 to 6 minutes or until egg whites are partially set. Let stand, covered, 3 to 4 minutes.

Carefully spoon eggs and sauce over English muffins. Yield: 4 servings (217 calories per serving).

PROTEIN 10.6 / FAT 6.4 / CARBOHYDRATE 29.3 / FIBER 1.6 / CHOLESTEROL 274 / SODIUM 409 / POTASSIUM 676

# CURRIED LAMB AND VEGETABLE MEDLEY

1½ pounds lean boneless lamb, cut into 1-inch cubes
½ cup chopped onion
1 tablespoon vegetable oil
1 clove garlic, minced
1 cup hot water
1 teaspoon minced fresh gingerroot
1 teaspoon chicken-flavored bouillon granules
1 teaspoon curry powder
½ teaspoon ground coriander
½ teaspoon dry mustard
½ teaspoon cumin seeds
¼ teaspoon ground cardamom
¼ teaspoon pepper
2 tablespoons water
2 teaspoons cornstarch
1 cup broccoli flowerets
1 sweet red pepper, cut into julienne strips
1 small yellow squash, cut into ¼-inch slices

Combine lamb, onion, vegetable oil, and garlic in a 3-quart baking dish. Cover with wax paper, and microwave at HIGH for 6 to 7 minutes or until meat is no longer pink, stirring every 2 minutes. Drain and pat dry with paper towels. Wipe pan drippings from dish with paper towels.

Return mixture to dish. Stir in 1 cup hot water and next 8 ingredients. Cover and microwave at MEDIUM (50% power) for 30 to 35 minutes, stirring twice. Combine 2 tablespoons water and cornstarch, stirring until smooth; stir into lamb mixture. Microwave at HIGH, uncovered, 2 to 3 minutes or until thickened, stirring once. Add broccoli, sweet red pepper, and squash. Cover and microwave at HIGH for 5 to 7 minutes or until vegetables are crisp-tender. Serve immediately. Yield: 6 servings (204 calories per serving).

PROTEIN 25.3 / FAT 8.7 / CARBOHYDRATE 5.4 / CHOLESTEROL 85 / IRON 2.6 / SODIUM 195 / CALCIUM 30

# PRIZE CHICKEN CUTLETS

---

**4 (6-ounce) chicken thighs, skinned and boned**
**½ teaspoon dried whole thyme**
**¼ teaspoon garlic powder**
**¼ teaspoon salt**
**¼ teaspoon pepper**
**1 cup sliced fresh mushrooms**
**½ cup chopped sweet red pepper**
**½ cup sliced green onions**
**¼ cup Chablis or other dry white wine**
**2 tablespoons grated Parmesan cheese**
**Green onion fans (optional)**

Place chicken thighs between 2 sheets of wax paper; flatten to ⅛-inch thickness using a meat mallet or rolling pin.

Combine thyme, garlic powder, salt, and pepper. Rub chicken or all sides with thyme mixture; let stand 5 minutes.

Arrange chicken thighs in a 1-quart casserole. Add mushrooms, sweet red pepper, green onions, and wine to chicken. Cover with heavy-duty plastic wrap and microwave at HIGH for 6 to 8 minutes or until chicken is done and vegetables are tender, rotating dish one-half turn after 3 minutes.

Remove chicken and vegetables to a serving platter. Sprinkle Parmesan cheese evenly over chicken. Garnish chicken with green onion fans, if desired. Yield: 4 servings (143 calories per serving).

PROTEIN 21.2 / FAT 4.8 / CARBOHYDRATE 3.1 / CHOLESTEROL 84 / IRON 2.0 / SODIUM 281 / CALCIUM 60

# TURKEY JOES

½ cup chopped onion
½ cup chopped celery
1 teaspoon vegetable oil
3 cups finely chopped cooked turkey (skinned before cooking and cooked without salt)
1 (8-ounce) can no-salt-added tomato sauce
1 (6-ounce) can no-salt-added tomato paste
2 tablespoons chopped fresh parsley
½ teaspoon chili powder
¼ teaspoon salt
¼ teaspoon ground cumin
⅛ teaspoon pepper
4 English muffins, split and toasted

Combine onion, celery, and vegetable oil in a 2-quart casserole. Cover with heavy-duty plastic wrap and microwave at HIGH for 2 to 3 minutes or until vegetables are tender. Drain vegetables, and pat dry with a paper towel. Wipe pan drippings from casserole with a paper towel.

Return vegetables to casserole; stir in turkey and next 7 ingredients. Cover and microwave at HIGH for 3 to 4 minutes or until thoroughly heated, stirring once. To serve, place ½ cup turkey mixture on each muffin half. Yield: 8 servings (215 calories per serving).

PROTEIN 19.5 / FAT 4.0 / CARBOHYDRATE 24.7 / CHOLESTEROL 40 / IRON 2.4 / SODIUM 302 / CALCIUM 81

# CHICKEN AND DUMPLINGS

1 cup thinly sliced carrots
1 cup peeled, cubed red potato
½ cup chopped onion
½ cup sliced celery
1 cup canned no-salt-added chicken broth, undiluted
¼ teaspoon salt
3 (6-ounce) skinned chicken breast halves
1 cup plus 1 tablespoon all-purpose flour, divided
½ cup water
2 teaspoons dried parsley flakes
1 teaspoon baking powder
½ teaspoon dried whole thyme
¼ teaspoon salt
2 tablespoons shortening
⅓ cup plus 1 tablespoon nonfat buttermilk

Combine first 6 ingredients in a 12- x 8- x 2-inch baking dish. Place chicken over vegetable mixture with thickest portions towards outside of dish. Cover with wax paper and microwave at HIGH for 12 minutes or until chicken is tender, rotating dish a half-turn after every 4 minutes. Remove chicken; bone and chop. Set aside.

Cover vegetable mixture with wax paper and microwave at HIGH for 3 minutes. Combine 1 tablespoon of the flour and the water, stirring well. Stir flour mixture into vegetable mixture. Cover and microwave for 4 minutes, stirring once. Stir in reserved chicken.

Combine remaining 1 cup flour, parsley, baking powder, thyme, and ¼ teaspoon salt. Cut in shortening with a pastry blender until mixture resembles coarse meal. Add buttermilk to dry ingredients, stirring with a fork just until moistened. Roll dough to ¼-inch thickness; cut into twelve 1½-inch rounds. Place flat side down over chicken mixture. Cover with wax paper; microwave at HIGH for 4 minutes, rotating dish a half-turn after 2 minutes. Let stand, covered, 5 minutes. Yield: 6 servings (241 calories per serving).

PROTEIN 20.2 / FAT 5.1 / CARBOHYDRATE 27.2 / CHOLESTEROL 39 / IRON 1.8 / SODIUM 345 / CALCIUM 60

# ROSEMARY GRILLED LAMB CHOPS

½ cup Chablis or other dry white wine
2 tablespoons lemon juice
1 tablespoon vegetable oil
4 cloves garlic, minced
2 teaspoons dried whole rosemary
⅛ teaspoon salt
¼ teaspoon pepper
6 (6-ounce) lamb loin chops (1-inch thick)
Vegetable cooking spray

Combine first 7 ingredients in an 11- x 7- x 2-inch baking dish, stirring well.

Trim fat from chops; place chops in baking dish. Cover and marinate in refrigerator at least 8 hours, turning chops occasionally.

Arrange chops with thickest portion towards outside of dish. Cover with wax paper and microwave at MEDIUM (50% power) for 8 minutes, turning chops over and rearranging after 4 minutes. Drain chops, reserving marinade.

Coat grill rack with cooking spray; place on grill over medium-hot coals. Place chops on rack, and cook 14 minutes or to desired degree of doneness, turning and basting frequently with reserved marinade. Serve immediately. Yield: 6 servings (264 calories per serving).

PROTEIN 33.9 / FAT 12.4 / CARBOHYDRATE 2.2 / CHOLESTEROL 119 / IRON 3.1 / SODIUM 178 / CALCIUM 32

# CHICKEN MOZZARELLA

½ cup whole wheat breadcrumbs
¼ cup wheat germ
8 (4-ounce) boneless chicken breast halves, skinned
½ cup skim milk
Vegetable cooking spray
2 teaspoons sesame or vegetable oil
1 (8-ounce) can no-salt-added tomato sauce
1 tablespoon minced fresh parsley
1 teaspoon dried whole basil
1 teaspoon dried whole oregano
⅛ teaspoon pepper
1 clove garlic, minced
½ cup (2-ounces) shredded mozzarella cheese

Combine breadcrumbs and wheat germ; set mixture aside.

Trim excess fat from chicken. Place chicken between 2 sheets of waxed paper, and flatten to ¼-inch thickness, using a meat mallet or rolling pin. Dip chicken in skim milk; dredge in breadcrumb mixture. Coat a large skillet with cooking spray; add sesame oil, and place over medium heat until hot. Add chicken to skillet, and cook until browned on both sides. Drain on paper towels.

Pour one third of tomato sauce in bottom of a 13- x 9- x 2-inch baking dish coated with cooking spray. Place chicken breasts in dish. Pour half of remaining tomato sauce over chicken; sprinkle with parsley, basil, oregano, pepper, garlic, and cheese. Top with remaining tomato sauce.

Microwave, uncovered, at HIGH for 8 to 10 minutes; rearrange chicken after 4 minutes. Cover with heavy-duty plastic wrap, and let stand 2 minutes. Yield: 8 servings (209 calories per serving).

PROTEIN 29.7 / FAT 6.3 / CARBOHYDRATES 7.9 / FIBER 0.7 / CHOLESTEROL 76 / SODIUM 135 / POTASSIUM 294

# ZUCCHINI-BEEF BURRITOS

¾ pound lean flank steak
½ cup oil-free Italian dressing
1 clove garlic, minced
6 (8-inch) flour tortillas
1 cup shredded zucchini
½ cup chopped green onions
6 cherry tomatoes, quartered
Vegetable cooking spray
1 (8-ounce) can no-salt-added tomato sauce
½ teaspoon chili powder
¼ teaspoon garlic powder
⅛ teaspoon onion powder
¼ cup (1 ounce) finely shredded Monterey Jack cheese
  with jalapeño peppers
¼ cup (1 ounce) finely shredded 40% less-fat Cheddar
  cheese

Partially freeze steak; trim fat from steak. Slice steak diagonally across grain into thin strips. Cut each strip in half lengthwise. Arrange in a 2½-quart shallow casserole. Combine dressing and garlic; pour over beef. Cover and marinate in refrigerator at least 2 hours.

Cover casserole with wax paper. Microwave at MEDIUM-HIGH (70% power) for 5 minutes; stir. Cover and microwave at MEDIUM-HIGH an additional 7 minutes or to desired degree of doneness, stirring after 3 minutes. Let stand, covered, 5 minutes. Drain and discard marinade.

Place tortillas between paper towels and microwave at HIGH for 40 seconds to 1 minute or until softened. Distribute prepared beef, zucchini, green onions, and tomato evenly down center of each tortilla. Roll up and place seam side up in a 13- x 9- x 2-inch baking dish that has been coated with cooking spray.

Combine tomato sauce, chili powder, garlic powder, and onion powder; stir well. Pour over burritos. Cover with wax paper. Microwave at MEDIUM-HIGH for 2 to 3 minutes or until thoroughly heated. Uncover; sprinkle with cheeses. Microwave, uncovered, at HIGH 1 to 2 minutes or until cheese melts. Serve immediately. Yield: 6 servings (313 calories per serving).

PROTEIN 17.8 / FAT 12.1 / CARBOHYDRATE 35.9 / CHOLESTEROL 34 / IRON 2.5 / SODIUM 197 / CALCIUM 122

# STUFFED CORNISH HENS

1½ cups cooked parboiled rice (cooked without salt or fat)
2 tablespoons minced fresh parsley
¼ teaspoon grated lemon rind
1 tablespoon plus 1½ teaspoons lemon juice
1 tablespoon plus 1½ teaspoons minced green onion
½ teaspoon chicken-flavored bouillon granules
¼ teaspoon celery seeds
¼ teaspoon pepper
2 (1¼-pound) Cornish hens, completely thawed and skinned
½ cup Chablis or other dry white wine
¼ cup water
1 teaspoon Worcestershire sauce
½ teaspoon poultry seasoning
¼ teaspoon chicken-flavored bouillon granules
¼ teaspoon paprika
⅛ teaspoon garlic powder

Combine first 8 ingredients in a medium bowl, stirring well; set aside.

Remove giblets from hens; reserve for use in another recipe. Rinse hens with cold water, and pat dry. Stuff hens with reserved rice mixture. Close cavities, and secure with wooden picks; truss. Twist the wing tips behind backs.

Place hens, breast side down, on a microwave rack. Place rack inside a 13- x 9- x 2-inch baking dish.

Combine Chablis, water, Worcestershire sauce, poultry seasoning, ¼ teaspoon bouillon granules, paprika, and garlic powder in a small bowl; pour one third of mixture over hens. Cover hens with a tent of waxed paper; microwave at HIGH for 10 minutes.

Turn hens breast side up, and give each a half turn on rack. Pour half of remaining wine mixture over hens. Cover with waxed paper tent; microwave at HIGH for 3 minutes.

Pour remaining wine mixture over hens; cover with waxed paper tent. Microwave at HIGH an additional 6 minutes or until juices run clear when hens are pierced with a fork between leg and thigh. Microwave meat thermometer should register 185° when inserted in meaty area between leg and thigh. Cover with aluminum foil, and let stand 4 to 6 minutes. Split hens in half with an electric knife and serve. Yield: 4 servings (272 calories per serving).

PROTEIN 30.8 / FAT 7.7 / CARBOHYDRATES 18.0 / FIBER 0.7 / CHOLESTEROL 90 / SODIUM 173 / POTASSIUM 344

# MEXICALI TACOS

½ pound ground chuck
¼ (1-pound) package raw ground turkey, thawed
2 tablespoons wheat germ, toasted
3 tablespoons reduced-calorie chili sauce
½ teaspoon ground cumin
½ teaspoon dried whole oregano
4 taco shells
1 cup shredded iceberg lettuce
½ cup chopped tomato

Crumble ground chuck and turkey into a 2-quart casserole. Cover with wax paper, and microwave at HIGH for 5 to 6 minutes or until meat is no longer pink, stirring every 2 minutes. Drain meat well; pat with paper towels to remove excess grease. Wipe drippings from casserole. Return meat to casserole; stir in wheat germ, chili sauce, cumin, and oregano. Cover and microwave at MEDIUM (50% power) for 3 to 4 minutes or until meat mixture is thoroughly heated.

Place taco shells in a circle on a paper plate. Microwave at HIGH for 45 to 60 seconds or until taco shells are thoroughly heated. Divide meat mixture evenly among warm taco shells. Divide shredded lettuce and chopped tomato evenly among taco shells. Yield: 4 servings (219 calories per serving).

PROTEIN 19.7 / FAT 11.3 / CARBOHYDRATE 10.3 / CHOLESTEROL 51 / IRON 2.6 / SODIUM 109 / CALCIUM 22

# COUNTRY CHICKEN WITH CREAMY GRAVY

¾ cup whole grain corn flakes cereal, crushed
½ teaspoon paprika
½ teaspoon poultry seasoning
¼ teaspoon dried whole thyme
¼ teaspoon salt
¼ teaspoon pepper
2 tablespoons evaporated skim milk
6 (4-ounce) skinned, boned chicken breast halves
Creamy Gravy (recipe follows)

Place cereal, paprika, poultry seasoning, thyme, salt, and pepper in a shallow dish, stirring well to combine. Pour evaporated skim milk into a shallow bowl. Dip chicken breast halves in milk; dredge in cereal mixture.

Place coated chicken breast halves in an 11- x 7- x 2-inch baking dish with thickest portions towards outside of dish. Cover with wax paper, and microwave at HIGH for 12 minutes or until chicken is done, rotating dish a half-turn every 4 minutes.

Remove chicken to a serving platter, and keep warm. Spoon Creamy Gravy evenly over chicken. Serve immediately. Yield: 6 servings (218 calories per serving).

## Creamy Gravy:

1 tablespoon margarine
1 tablespoon all-purpose flour
½ cup evaporated skim milk
¼ cup canned no-salt-added chicken broth, undiluted
1 teaspoon dry sherry
¼ teaspoon salt
¼ teaspoon ground white pepper
2 tablespoons chopped fresh chives

Place margarine in a 4-cup glass measure; microwave, uncovered, at HIGH for 30 seconds or until melted. Add flour; stir until smooth. Gradually add milk, broth, and sherry; stir until smooth. Microwave at HIGH for 3 to 5 minutes or until thickened, stirring once. Stir in salt, pepper, and chives. Serve immediately. Yield: 1 cup.

PROTEIN 29.7 / FAT 3.6 / CARBOHYDRATE 15.5 / CHOLESTEROL 67 / IRON 1.5 / SODIUM 416 / CALCIUM 100

# HAM AND GRITS PIE

⅓ cup quick-cooking grits, uncooked
1 cup hot water
1 cup minced lean cooked ham
¾ cup evaporated skim milk
½ cup (2 ounces) shredded 40% less-fat Cheddar cheese
3 eggs, beaten
3 tablespoons chopped fresh chives
¼ teaspoon garlic powder
¼ teaspoon dry mustard
¼ teaspoon hot sauce
Vegetable cooking spray
½ cup whole wheat flakes cereal, crushed
½ teaspoon paprika

Combine grits and the water in a 2-quart casserole. Microwave, uncovered, at HIGH for 5 minutes, stirring after 3½ minutes. Combine grits, ham, and next 7 ingredients in a bowl. Pour mixture into a 9-inch glass pie plate that has been coated with cooking spray. Sprinkle cereal and paprika over top of mixture. Place pie plate in microwave oven on an inverted saucer. Microwave, uncovered, at MEDIUM-HIGH (70% power) for 13 to 15 minutes or just until center is set, giving dish a quarter-turn after every 4 minutes. Let stand 10 minutes. Yield: 6 servings (173 calories per serving).

PROTEIN 13.6 / FAT 5.4 / CARBOHYDRATE 18.8 / CHOLESTEROL 117 / IRON 1.2 / SODIUM 533 / CALCIUM 175

# BARBECUED CHICKEN

3 tablespoons brown sugar
3 tablespoons reduced-calorie catsup
2 tablespoons reduced-calorie chili sauce
1 tablespoon vinegar
2 teaspoons lemon juice
2 teaspoons low-sodium Worcestershire sauce
½ teaspoon salt
¼ teaspoon pepper
6 (4-ounce) skinned, boned chicken breast halves

Combine first 8 ingredients in a 2-cup glass measure. Microwave, uncovered, at HIGH for 1½ minutes or until mixture boils; set aside.

Arrange chicken in a 12- x 8- x 2-inch baking dish with thickest portions towards outside of dish. Cover with wax paper, and microwave at HIGH for 10 minutes. Drain off drippings, and rearrange chicken. Brush chicken with sauce. Cover and microwave at HIGH for 9 to 10 minutes or until chicken is done, rearranging chicken and brushing with sauce after 5 minutes. Let stand 2 minutes. Yield: 6 servings (163 calories per serving).

PROTEIN 25.7 / FAT 2.9 / CARBOHYDRATE 6.4 / CHOLESTEROL 70 / IRON 1.0 / SODIUM 270 / CALCIUM 18

# SOUTHERN PECAN CATFISH

½ cup corn flake crumbs
¼ teaspoon salt
⅛ teaspoon paprika
⅛ teaspoon pepper
2 tablespoons finely chopped pecans
4 (4-ounce) farm-raised catfish fillets
2 egg whites, beaten
1 tablespoon margarine
Lemon twists (optional)
Fresh parsley sprigs (optional)

Combine cereal crumbs, salt, paprika, pepper, and pecans; stir well.

Rinse fillets with cold water; pat dry. Dip in egg white; dredge in crumb mixture.

Arrange fillets in an 11- x 7- x 2-inch baking dish with thickest portions to the outside of dish.

Place margarine in a 1-cup glass measure. Microwave at HIGH for 35 seconds or until melted; drizzle over fish. Cover with wax paper; microwave at HIGH for 4 to 6 minutes or until fish flakes easily when tested with a fork, rearranging after 3 minutes. Let stand 1 minute. If desired, garnish with lemon twists and parsley sprigs. Yield: 4 servings (246 calories per serving).

PROTEIN 23.7 / FAT 10.2 / CARBOHYDRATE 14.1 / CHOLESTEROL 66 / IRON 2.2 / SODIUM 409 / CALCIUM 55

# CHICKEN TERIYAKI

⅓ cup Chablis or other dry white wine
¼ cup low-sodium soy sauce
3 tablespoons unsweetened pineapple juice
2 tablespoons honey
4 (4-ounce) skinned, boned chicken breast halves
1 (8-ounce) can sliced water chestnuts, drained
1 tablespoon water
2½ teaspoons cornstarch
2 cups hot cooked long-grain rice (cooked without salt or
    fat)

Combine wine, soy sauce, pineapple juice, and honey; stir well. Set aside.

Trim fat from chicken. Rinse with cold, running water and pat dry. Place chicken in an 11- x 7- x 2-inch baking dish with thickest portions towards outside of dish. Pour wine mixture over chicken. Cover and marinate in refrigerator 2 hours, turning occasionally.

Top chicken with water chestnuts. Cover with wax paper and microwave at HIGH for 8 to 10 minutes or until chicken is tender, rearranging after 5 minutes.

Remove chicken from marinade, reserving marinade. Set chicken aside, and keep warm.

Combine the water and cornstarch in a glass measure, stirring well. Gradually stir in reserved marinade. Microwave at HIGH for 3 to 4 minutes or until thickened. Arrange chicken over hot cooked rice. Spoon sauce evenly over chicken. Yield: 4 servings (355 calories per serving).

PROTEIN 30.1 / FAT 1.6 / CARBOHYDRATE 52.4 / CHOLESTEROL 66 / IRON 2.6 / SODIUM 681 / CALCIUM 33

# SLOPPY JOES

1 pound ground chuck
½ cup chopped onion
¼ cup chopped celery
2 cloves garlic, minced
1 (8-ounce) can no-salt-added tomato sauce
1 (6-ounce) can no-salt-added tomato paste
1 tablespoon vinegar
2 teaspoons sugar
½ teaspoon dry mustard
½ teaspoon salt
3 English muffins, split and toasted

Combine ground chuck, onion, celery, and garlic in a 2½-quart baking dish. Cover and microwave at HIGH for 5½ to 6½ minutes or until meat is no longer pink, stirring every 2 minutes. Drain and pat dry with paper towels. Wipe pan drippings from dish with a paper towel.

Return meat to baking dish; stir in tomato sauce and next 5 ingredients. Cover and microwave at HIGH for 3 to 4 minutes or until thoroughly heated, stirring once. To serve, place ½ cup meat mixture over each English muffin half. Yield: 6 servings (277 calories per serving).

PROTEIN 19.3 / FAT 10.0 / CARBOHYDRATE 28.6 / CHOLESTEROL 46 / IRON 3.0 / SODIUM 416 / CALCIUM 75

# LEMON FLOUNDER

**3 medium lemons, thinly sliced**
**4 (4-ounce) flounder fillets**
**1 tablespoon margarine**

Arrange lemon slices on a 12-inch round glass platter. Rinse fish with cold water, and pat dry. Arrange fillets on lemon slices with thickest end of fillet at outer edges of platter. Place margarine in a 1-cup glass measure. Microwave at HIGH for 35 seconds or until melted. Drizzle margarine over fish.

Cover with heavy-duty plastic wrap, and vent. Microwave at HIGH for 6 to 8 minutes or until fish flakes easily when tested with a fork, rotating platter after 3 minutes. Let stand 1 minute. Drain off excess liquid. Serve immediately. Yield: 4 servings (131 calories per serving).

PROTEIN 19.9 / FAT 4.0 / CARBOHYDRATE 8.6 / CHOLESTEROL 57 / IRON 1.4 / SODIUM 124 / CALCIUM 64

# SAFARI CHICKEN STEW

1 (2-pound) broiler fryer, cut up and skinned
1 tablespoon olive oil
1 clove garlic, minced
2 medium onions, sliced
2 medium carrots, scraped and sliced
2 small zucchini, sliced
¾ cup cubed turnips
2 tablespoons raisins
½ cup water
½ teaspoon chicken-flavored bouillon granules
½ teaspoon lemon juice
½ teaspoon ground cinnamon
½ teaspoon ground cumin
⅛ teaspoon crushed red pepper

Trim excess fat from chicken. Rinse chicken with cold water, and pat dry. Arrange chicken pieces on a 12-inch round glass platter with meatier portions towards outside of dish. Combine olive oil and garlic in a small bowl; sprinkle over chicken. Cover with heavy-duty plastic wrap and vent; microwave at HIGH for 7 to 8 minutes, rotating platter a half-turn after 3 minutes.

Transfer chicken to a 3-quart casserole. Add onions and next 4 ingredients; set aside. Combine the water and bouillon granules; stir in remaining ingredients. Pour bouillon mixture over reserved chicken and vegetables. Cover with lid; microwave at HIGH for 14 to 15 minutes or until chicken and vegetables are tender, rotating dish after 7 minutes. Let stand, covered, 5 minutes. Yield: 4 servings (249 calories per serving).

PROTEIN 25.4 / FAT 9.8 / CARBOHYDRATE 15.0 / CHOLESTEROL 72 / IRON 2.0 / SODIUM 150 / CALCIUM 60

# SOLE EN PAPILLOTE WITH GARDEN VEGETABLES

1 tablespoon margarine
1 medium-size sweet red pepper, seeded and sliced
2 medium carrots, cut into julienne strips
⅔ cup fresh broccoli flowerets
1 clove garlic, crushed
4 (4-ounce) sole fillets
2 teaspoons lemon juice
¼ teaspoon paprika
⅛ teaspoon pepper

Place margarine in a 1-quart casserole. Microwave at HIGH for 20 seconds or until melted. Add red pepper, carrots, broccoli, and garlic; cover and microwave at HIGH for 2 to 3 minutes or until crisp tender, stirring once; set aside.

Cut 4 16- x 12-inch pieces of parchment paper; cut each into a large heart shape. Fold in half; open out flat. Place a fillet along center fold on each sheet of paper. Sprinkle fillets with lemon juice, paprika, and pepper.

Top each fillet with equal amounts of vegetable mixture. Fold paper edges over to seal securely. Place 2 pouches on a microwave-safe 12-inch platter. Microwave at HIGH for 3 to 4 minutes; set aside. Repeat with remaining pouches. Transfer pouches to serving plates. Cut openings in pouches before serving. Yield: 4 servings (135 calories per serving).

PROTEIN 20.0 / FAT 4.0 / CARBOHYDRATES 4.3 / FIBER 0.8 / CHOLESTEROL 57 / SODIUM 136 / POTASSIUM 553

# SHRIMP IN OYSTER SAUCE

1 tablespoon dry sherry
1 tablespoon water
2 teaspoons vegetable oil, divided
1 pound fresh, medium-size shrimp, peeled and deveined
1 (8-ounce) can sliced water chestnuts, drained
1 cup sliced celery
1 medium-size sweet red pepper, seeded and cut into strips
2 cloves garlic, minced
1 teaspoon minced fresh gingerroot
½ cup water
1 tablespoon cornstarch
1 tablespoon oyster sauce
1 teaspoon sugar
1 teaspoon reduced-sodium soy sauce
½ teaspoon chicken-flavored bouillon granules
½ cup diagonally sliced green onions
Green onion fan (optional)

Combine sherry, 1 tablespoon water, and 1 teaspoon vegetable oil in a shallow dish. Add shrimp; toss gently. Let stand 20 minutes.

Combine remaining 1 teaspoon vegetable oil, water chestnuts, celery, red pepper, garlic, and gingerroot in a 2-quart casserole. Microwave, uncovered, at HIGH 2 to 3 minutes. Drain shrimp, discarding liquid. Add shrimp to casserole; stir well. Microwave, uncovered, at HIGH 3 to 4 minutes or until shrimp are no longer pink, stirring after 2 minutes. Cover, and set aside.

Combine ½ cup water and next 5 ingredients in a 2-cup glass measure, stirring well. Microwave, uncovered, at HIGH 2 minutes, stirring after 1 minute. Add to reserved shrimp mixture. Stir in green onions. Microwave, uncovered, at HIGH 1 to 2 minutes or until thoroughly heated. Garnish with green onion fan, if desired. Yield: 4 servings (149 calories per serving).

PROTEIN 16.6 / FAT 3.2 / CARBOHYDRATE 12.4 / CHOLESTEROL 128 / IRON 2.5 / SODIUM 395 / CALCIUM 80

# SHREDDED CHICKEN SALAD

2 (4-ounce) boneless chicken breast halves, skinned
4 large romaine lettuce leaves
2 cups shredded iceberg lettuce
1 cup thinly sliced cucumber
½ cup shredded zucchini
1 tablespoon olive oil
1 clove garlic, minced
¼ teaspoon dried whole oregano
¼ cup red wine vinegar
3 tablespoons water
⅛ teaspoon pepper
1 tablespoon grated Parmesan cheese

Trim excess fat from chicken. Rinse chicken with cold water, and pat dry. Place in a 1-quart glass baking dish. Cover with heavy-duty plastic wrap and vent; microwave at HIGH for 4 to 6 minutes or until chicken is tender, turning chicken and rotating dish a half-turn after 2 minutes. Let cool to room temperature. Shred chicken into bite-size pieces, and set aside.

Arrange romaine leaves on a serving platter. Top with shredded iceberg, cucumber, zucchini, and reserved chicken.

Place olive oil in a 1-cup glass measure. Microwave, uncovered, at HIGH for 30 seconds to 1 minute. Stir in garlic and oregano. Microwave at HIGH for 30 seconds. Stir in vinegar, water, and pepper. Pour mixture over salad. Sprinkle with Parmesan cheese. Yield: 4 servings (123 calories per serving).

PROTEIN 14.7 / FAT 5.4 / CARBOHYDRATE 3.3 / CHOLESTEROL 36 / IRON 1.2 / SODIUM 63 / CALCIUM 52

# CONTINENTAL SALMON LOAF

2 (4-ounce) salmon steaks, about ¾-inch thick
½ cup thinly sliced green onions
1 tablespoon olive oil
1 tablespoon all-purpose flour
1 cup skim milk
2 eggs, beaten
½ teaspoon dried whole dillweed
¼ teaspoon salt
¼ teaspoon coarsely ground pepper
1 tablespoon finely chopped pistachio nuts
1 small onion, thinly sliced
1 lemon, cut into wedges
Fresh dill sprigs (optional)

Rinse salmon with cold water, and pat dry. Arrange in a 1-quart casserole; cover with heavy-duty plastic wrap, and vent. Microwave at HIGH 4 minutes or until fish flakes easily when tested with a fork, turning steaks after 2 minutes. Let cool to room temperature. Remove skin, and flake fish from bones. Set aside.

Combine green onions and olive oil in casserole. Microwave, uncovered, at HIGH 1 to 1½ minutes or until onions are tender. Stir in flour. Gradually stir in milk. Microwave, uncovered, at MEDIUM (50% power) 9 to 12 minutes or until thickened, stirring every 2 minutes. Add reserved salmon, eggs, dillweed, salt, and pepper; stir gently. Cover casserole with wax paper, and place in oven on top of an inverted saucer. Microwave at MEDIUM-HIGH (70% power) 8 to 10 minutes or until set, rotating casserole a half-turn after 4 minutes. Let casserole stand, covered, 5 minutes. Chill thoroughly.

Invert chilled salmon mixture onto a serving plate. Sprinkle with pistachio nuts. Separate onion slices into rings, and arrange with lemon wedges around salmon. Garnish with dill sprigs, if desired. To serve, cut into slices or wedges. Yield: 4 servings (239 calories per serving).

PROTEIN 18.5 / FAT 14.0 / CARBOHYDRATE 11.4 / CHOLESTEROL 157 / IRON 1.9 / SODIUM 242 / CALCIUM 228

# SHISH KABOBS

½ pound lean boneless lamb
2 tablespoons white wine vinegar
2 tablespoons water
1 tablespoon dry sherry
2 teaspoons chopped fresh parsley
1 teaspoon sugar
¾ teaspoon dried whole rosemary, crushed
⅛ teaspoon garlic salt
⅛ teaspoon pepper
1 small green pepper, seeded and cut into 8 pieces
6 medium-size fresh mushrooms
4 cherry tomatoes

Trim excess fat from lamb; cut into 1-inch cubes. Place lamb in a 9-inch square baking dish. Combine vinegar, water, sherry, parsley, sugar, rosemary, garlic salt, and pepper in a small bowl, stirring well; pour over lamb. Cover and refrigerate 8 hours or overnight.

Place green pepper on a microwave-safe plate; cover and microwave at HIGH for 2 minutes. Drain lamb, discarding marinade. Alternate lamb and vegetables on four 10-inch wooden skewers. Place skewers on a microwave-safe roasting rack; cover with waxed paper. Microwave at MEDIUM (50% power) for 10 to 12 minutes, or until desired degree of doneness, rearranging kabobs after 5 minutes. Yield: 2 servings (216 calories per serving).

PROTEIN 26.1 / FAT 6.8 / CARBOHYDRATES 10.8 / FIBER 1.7 / CHOLESTEROL 85 / SODIUM 201 / POTASSIUM 681

# CHEESY PITA SALAD SANDWICHES

1 medium tomato, coarsely chopped
½ cup sliced cucumber
½ cup alfalfa sprouts
¼ cup chopped sweet red pepper
¼ cup chopped green pepper
¼ cup chopped celery
⅛ teaspoon coarsely ground pepper
¼ cup reduced-calorie Italian salad dressing
½ cup (2 ounces) shredded Swiss cheese
2 (6-inch) whole wheat pita bread rounds, cut in half
  crosswise

Combine first 8 ingredients in a medium bowl; toss well. Set aside.

Divide Swiss cheese evenly into pocket bread halves; cover with paper towels, and microwave at MEDIUM-HIGH (70% power) for 30 seconds to 1 minute or until cheese melts.

Open sandwiches, and stuff with equal amounts of vegetable mixture. Serve immediately. Yield: 4 servings (139 calories per serving).

PROTEIN 6.2 / FAT 4.6 / CARBOHYDRATES 17.6 / FIBER 1.9 / CHOLESTEROL 14 / SODIUM 310 / POTASSIUM 246

# RICE
# AND COUSCOUS

## SAVORY RICE

1⅔ cups water
¼ cup grated onion
1 teaspoon margarine
¼ teaspoon salt
¼ teaspoon pepper
1½ cups instant rice, uncooked
1 medium tomato, peeled, seeded, and chopped
2 tablespoons chopped fresh parsley
2 tablespoons unsalted sunflower kernels, toasted

Combine first 5 ingredients in a 2-quart casserole; stir in rice and tomato. Cover with heavy-duty plastic wrap, and microwave at HIGH for 8 to 10 minutes or until liquid is absorbed. Let stand 2 minutes. Fluff rice with a fork; sprinkle parsley and sunflower kernels over rice. Yield: 6 servings (130 calories per ½-cup serving).

PROTEIN 3.3 / FAT 3.1 / CARBOHYDRATE 22.4 / CHOLESTEROL 0 / IRON 1.3 / SODIUM 107 / CALCIUM 15

# MEXICAN RICE

1⅔ cups water
½ teaspoon dry mustard
½ teaspoon beef-flavored bouillon granules
1½ cups instant rice, uncooked
¼ cup chopped green pepper
1 (4-ounce) can chopped green chiles, undrained

Combine the water, dry mustard, and bouillon granules in a 2-quart casserole. Stir in rice and chopped green pepper. Cover with heavy-duty plastic wrap, and microwave at HIGH for 8 to 10 minutes or until liquid is absorbed. Let stand 3 minutes. Stir in chopped green chiles. Fluff with a fork before serving. Yield: 6 servings (97 calories per ½-cup serving).

PROTEIN 2.0 / FAT 0.2 / CARBOHYDRATE 21.1 / CHOLESTEROL 0 / IRON 0.9 / SODIUM 79 / CALCIUM 3

# BROWN RICE WITH PECANS

1¾ cups hot water
¼ cup unsweetened orange juice
⅔ cup long grain brown rice, uncooked
1 teaspoon chicken-flavored bouillon granules
1 tablespoon chopped fresh mint
1 tablespoon chopped fresh parsley
½ teaspoon grated orange rind
⅛ teaspoon pepper
2 tablespoons chopped pecans, toasted

Combine water and orange juice in a 2-quart casserole. Cover with lid and microwave at HIGH for 4 minutes or until boiling. Stir in rice and bouillon granules. Microwave, covered, at MEDIUM (50% power) for 45 minutes or until liquid is absorbed. Let stand, covered, 5 minutes. Add mint, parsley, orange rind, and pepper;

stir well. Cover and chill thoroughly. Stir in pecans just before serving. Yield: 4 servings (145 calories per serving).

PROTEIN 2.8 / FAT 3.2 / CARBOHYDRATE 26.5 / CHOLESTEROL 0 / IRON 0.7 / SODIUM 99 / CALCIUM 16

# COUSCOUS WITH PARSLEY

½ cup water
3 ounces couscous
1 tablespoon olive oil
¼ teaspoon ground turmeric
2 tablespoons chopped fresh parsley

Place the water in a 4-cup glass measure. Microwave at HIGH for 1½ minutes or until water boils; stir in remaining ingredients. Cover with heavy-duty plastic wrap, and vent; microwave at HIGH for 1½ to 2 minutes or until liquid is absorbed. Let stand 2 to 3 minutes. Fluff couscous with a fork before serving. Yield: 4 servings (51 calories per serving).

PROTEIN 0.8 / FAT 3.4 / CARBOHYDRATE 4.5 / CHOLESTEROL 0 / IRON 0.3 / SODIUM 1 / CALCIUM 5

# SESAME-GINGER RICE

2 cups hot water
¼ teaspoon salt
⅔ cup long-grain rice, uncooked
½ cup diced carrots
¾ teaspoon minced fresh gingerroot
2½ teaspoons sesame oil

Place the water and salt in a 2-quart casserole. Microwave at HIGH for 3 to 3½ minutes or until boiling. Add rice, carrots, and gingerroot; stir well. Cover with lid, and microwave at HIGH for 5 minutes. Reduce to MEDIUM (50% power), and microwave 14 minutes or until liquid is absorbed. Stir in sesame oil; let stand 5 minutes. Fluff with a fork, and serve immediately. Yield: 4 servings (143 calories per serving).

PROTEIN 2.2 / FAT 3.0 / CARBOHYDRATE 26.2 / CHOLESTEROL 0 / IRON 1.0 / SODIUM 153 / CALCIUM 12

# HERBED-PARSLEY RICE

1 medium onion, chopped
2 tablespoons water
1 teaspoon margarine
1¼ cups hot water
⅔ cup parboiled rice, uncooked
1 teaspoon chicken-flavored bouillon granules
¼ teaspoon dried whole basil
¼ teaspoon dried whole thyme
¼ teaspoon pepper
½ cup chopped fresh parsley

Combine onion, 2 tablespoons water, and margarine in a 2-quart casserole. Cover with heavy-duty plastic wrap, and microwave at HIGH for 1½ to 2 minutes or until onion is tender. Add 1¼ cups hot water, rice, bouillon granules, basil, thyme, and pepper; stir well. Cover with heavy-duty plastic wrap, and microwave at HIGH for 4 to 5 minutes. Reduce power to MEDIUM (50% power), and microwave an additional 12 to 14 minutes or until liquid is absorbed. Stir in parsley; let stand, covered, 8 minutes. Fluff with a fork, and serve immediately. Yield: 4 servings (145 calories per serving).

PROTEIN 2.9 / FAT 1.3 / CARBOHYDRATE 29.9 / FIBER 1.2 / CHOLESTEROL 0 / SODIUM 112 / POTASSIUM 127


# CURRIED RICE

---

⅓ **cup water**
2 **tablespoons chopped green onion**
⅓ **cup water**
⅓ **cup parboiled rice, uncooked**
½ **teaspoon chicken-flavored bouillon granules**
¼ **teaspoon curry powder**
**Dash of pepper**
**Green onion fans (optional)**

Combine ⅓ cup water and green onion in a 1-quart casserole. Cover and microwave at HIGH for 1 to 1½ minutes. Add ⅓ cup water, rice, bouillon granules, curry powder, and pepper; stir well. Cover and microwave at HIGH for 2½ to 3 minutes or until water boils; stir well. Cover; microwave at MEDIUM (50% power) for 10 to 12 minutes or until liquid is absorbed. Let stand 4 minutes. Garnish with green onion fans, if desired. Yield: 2 servings (115 calories per serving).

PROTEIN 2.3 / FAT 0.3 / CARBOHYDRATE 25.9 / FIBER 0.3 / CHOLESTEROL 0 / SODIUM 99 / POTASSIUM 74

# VEGETABLES

---

## CILANTRO-SEASONED CORN

---

3 cups fresh corn, cut from cob
¼ cup water
¼ cup chopped fresh cilantro
¼ teaspoon salt
¼ teaspoon cumin seeds
⅛ teaspoon pepper
1 medium tomato, peeled, seeded, and chopped

Combine first 6 ingredients in a 2-quart baking dish; stir well. Cover with wax paper, and microwave at HIGH for 6 to 8 minutes. Stir in tomato; cover and microwave at HIGH for 1 to 2 minutes or until corn is tender. Yield: 6 servings (72 calories per ½-cup serving).

PROTEIN 2.8 / FAT 1.0 / CARBOHYDRATE 15.8 / CHOLESTEROL 0 / IRON 0.7 / SODIUM 111 / CALCIUM 9

# CORN AND CELERY MINGLE

¼ cup sliced green onions
1 tablespoon reduced-calorie margarine
2 tablespoons chopped hickory smoke-flavored almonds,
    toasted
1 teaspoon lemon juice
1½ cups sliced celery
¼ cup water
1 (10-ounce) package frozen whole kernel corn

Place green onions and margarine in a 2-cup glass measure. Cover with wax paper, and microwave at HIGH for 2 minutes, stirring once. Add almonds and lemon juice, stirring well, set aside.

Place celery and the water in a 1½-quart casserole. Cover with heavy-duty plastic wrap, and microwave at HIGH for 3 minutes. Add corn; cover and microwave at HIGH for 6 to 7 minutes or until vegetables are crisp-tender, stirring once. Add reserved nut mixture, stirring well. Yield: 6 servings (77 calories per ½-cup serving).

PROTEIN 2.5 / FAT 3.2 / CARBOHYDRATE 11.6 / CHOLESTEROL 0 / IRON 0.5 / SODIUM 71 / CALCIUM 19

# LEMONY BABY CARROTS

1 (16-ounce) package baby carrots, scraped
¼ cup water
1 tablespoon lemon juice
1 teaspoon grated lemon rind
½ teaspoon dried whole dillweed
¼ teaspoon ground white pepper
⅛ teaspoon chicken-flavored bouillon granules

Combine all ingredients in a 1½-quart casserole; stir well. Cover with heavy-duty plastic wrap, and microwave at HIGH for 8 to 10 minutes or until crisp-tender, stirring after 4 minutes. Yield: 4 servings (37 calories per ½-cup serving).

PROTEIN 0.9 / FAT 0.2 / CARBOHYDRATE 8.8 / CHOLESTEROL 0 / IRON 0.5 / SODIUM 78 / CALCIUM 25

# MINTED PEAS AND CARROTS

¼ cup thinly sliced green onions
1 (16-ounce) package frozen green peas and carrots
3 tablespoons water
¼ cup chopped fresh mint leaves
⅛ teaspoon salt
⅛ teaspoon pepper
Fresh mint sprigs (optional)

Place first 3 ingredients in a 1-quart casserole. Cover with heavy-duty plastic wrap; microwave at HIGH for 5 to 8 minutes or until tender, stirring after 3 minutes. Stir in remaining ingredients. Garnish with mint sprigs, if desired. Yield: 6 servings (53 calories per ½-cup serving).

PROTEIN 3.3 / FAT 0.3 / CARBOHYDRATE 9.8 / CHOLESTEROL 0 / IRON 1.2 / SODIUM 125 / CALCIUM 25

# CANDIED SWEET POTATOES

2 large sweet potatoes (1¾ pounds)
3 tablespoons brown sugar
1 tablespoon margarine
1 tablespoon unsweetened orange juice

Wash sweet potatoes and pat dry; prick each sweet potato several times with a fork. Arrange sweet potatoes 1 inch apart on a layer of paper towels in microwave oven. Microwave, uncovered, at HIGH for 8 to 10 minutes or until sweet potatoes are tender, turning and rearranging potatoes after 4 minutes. Let potatoes stand 5 minutes.

Peel sweet potatoes and cut into ½-inch slices. Combine brown sugar and margarine in a 2-quart casserole. Microwave, uncovered, at HIGH for 1 to 1½ minutes or until sugar and margarine melt, stirring after 1 minute. Stir in orange juice. Add sweet potato slices, and toss gently. Cover with wax paper and microwave at HIGH for 1 to 2 minutes or until potatoes are thoroughly heated. Toss gently before serving. Serve immediately. Yield: 4 servings (158 calories per serving).

PROTEIN 1.7 / FAT 3.2 / CARBOHYDRATE 31.3 / CHOLESTEROL 0 / IRON 0.8 / SODIUM 49 / CALCIUM 29

# GARDEN CORN AND OKRA

¾ cup fresh corn
¾ cup sliced fresh okra
⅓ cup chopped green pepper
1 small onion, chopped
1 tablespoon water
1 teaspoon margarine
1 teaspoon sugar
½ teaspoon salt
⅛ teaspoon pepper
1 medium tomato, chopped
⅛ teaspoon hot sauce

Combine corn, okra, green pepper, onion, water, margarine, sugar, salt, and pepper in a 1-quart baking dish, tossing well. Cover with wax paper and microwave at HIGH for 8 to 10 minutes, stirring at 3-minute intervals. Add chopped tomato and hot sauce. Cover and microwave at HIGH for 1½ to 2 minutes or until mixture is thoroughly heated. Yield: 4 servings (65 calories per ½-cup serving).

PROTEIN 2.1 / FAT 1.5 / CARBOHYDRATE 12.5 / CHOLESTEROL 0 / IRON 0.8 / SODIUM 315 / CALCIUM 30

# HERBED CORN ON THE COB

**6 ears fresh corn**
**2 tablespoons margarine, softened**
**1 teaspoon dried salad herbs**

Pull back husks from corn, leaving husks attached at base of cob; remove silks. Rinse corn and pat dry. Pull husks up over corn. Rinse corn in husks; do not drain. Arrange corn on paper towels in microwave oven. Cover with wax paper. Microwave at HIGH for 16 to 18 minutes, rearranging after 8 minutes. Let stand 5 minutes; remove husks.

Combine margarine and salad herbs; spread 1 teaspoon margarine mixture over each ear of corn. Yield: 6 servings (100 calories per serving).

PROTEIN 2.0 / FAT 4.6 / CARBOHYDRATE 15.3 / CHOLESTEROL 0 / IRON 0.6 / SODIUM 55 / CALCIUM 10


# DILLED NEW POTATO HALVES

**8 small new potatoes (1 pound)**
**½ cup plain low-fat yogurt**
**1 tablespoon horseradish**
**⅛ teaspoon dried whole dillweed**
**2 tablespoons chopped fresh chives**

Rinse potatoes and pat dry. Prick potatoes several times with a fork, and place in a ring on a paper towel in microwave oven. Microwave at HIGH 6 to 7 minutes, turning over after 3½ minutes. Let stand 5 minutes.

Cut potatoes in half lengthwise; set aside. Combine yogurt, horseradish, and dillweed in a small bowl; stir well. Spoon 1 teaspoon yogurt mixture onto each potato half. Sprinkle with chives. Serve at room temperature. Yield: 4 servings (104 calories per serving).

PROTEIN 4.1 / FAT 0.6 / CARBOHYDRATE 21.3 / CHOLESTEROL 2 / IRON 1.6 / SODIUM 32 / CALCIUM 71

# FRESH TOMATOES WITH SPINACH SAUCE

¾ cup torn fresh spinach
¼ cup loosely packed fresh basil leaves
¼ cup low-fat buttermilk
2 tablespoons chopped green onions
1 tablespoon reduced-calorie mayonnaise
1 clove garlic, minced
3 medium tomatoes, cut into ¼-inch slices

Place spinach in a 1-quart casserole. Cover with heavy-duty plastic wrap and vent; microwave at HIGH for 30 seconds to 1 minute. Drain spinach well. Combine spinach, basil, and next 4 ingredients in container of an electric blender or food processor. Process until smooth. Cover and chill thoroughly.

Arrange tomato slices on a serving platter. Top with chilled spinach mixture. Yield: 4 servings (43 calories per serving).

PROTEIN 2.0 / FAT 1.5 / CARBOHYDRATE 6.5 / CHOLESTEROL 1 / IRON 0.9 / SODIUM 53 / CALCIUM 42

# SPAGHETTI SQUASH WITH SUMMER VEGETABLES

1 (3-pound) spaghetti squash
¼ cup water
½ teaspoon chicken-flavored bouillon granules
¼ cup hot water
2 medium zucchini, sliced
1 medium-size yellow squash, sliced
1 medium carrot, scraped and grated
½ cup chopped green pepper
¼ cup sliced green onion
3 tablespoons chopped fresh parsley
3 tablespoons grated Parmesan cheese
¼ teaspoon pepper

Wash spaghetti squash, and cut in half lengthwise; remove and discard seeds. Place squash, cut side down, in a 13- x 9- x 2-inch baking dish; add ¼ cup water to dish. Cover with heavy-duty plastic wrap, and microwave at HIGH for 20 to 22 minutes, rotating and rearranging at 8-minute intervals. Let stand, covered, 5 minutes. Drain spaghetti squash, and cool. Remove 4 cups spaghetti-like strands using a fork, and set aside. Reserve any remaining spaghetti squash for use in other recipes.

Combine bouillon granules and ¼ cup hot water in a 12- x 8- x 2-inch baking dish; stir until bouillon granules are dissolved, and set aside. Combine zucchini squash, yellow squash, carrot, green pepper, green onion, and reserved 4 cups spaghetti squash in a large bowl. Toss well to combine ingredients, and transfer to baking dish containing bouillon mixture. Sprinkle chopped parsley, Parmesan cheese, and pepper evenly over squash mixture.

Cover vegetable mixture with heavy-duty plastic wrap, and microwave at HIGH for 6 to 8 minutes, stirring at 3-minute intervals. Let stand, covered, 2 minutes. Yield: 8 servings (47 calories per serving).

PROTEIN 2.1 / FAT 0.9 / CARBOHYDRATE 8.5 / FIBER 1.8 / CHOLESTEROL 1 / SODIUM 78 / POTASSIUM 260

*Country Chicken with Creamy Gravy (page 25), Corn and Celery Mingle (page 46), fruit salad, and Raspberry Chiffon Pie (page 56).*

*An eye-catching meal accompaniment— New Potato Halves (page 50).*

*An elegant but easy dinner features Shish Kabobs (page 38) and Curried Rice (page 44).*

*Our Southwestern Dinner begins on a lively note with a hearty serving of Creamy Green Chile Soup (page 2).*

*Enjoy Creole Eggs (page 15) with Glazed Apples (page 54) for a fast but delicious breakfast.*

*Celebrate any occasion by serving Sole en Papillote with Garden Vegetables (page 34).*

*Shrimp in Oyster Sauce (page 35) and Sesame-Ginger Rice (page 43).*

*Bite into Cheesy Pita Salad Sandwiches (page 39) to taste the melted cheese inside.*

*Rum-Pineapple Boat (page 62) is an easy but impressive way to serve fruit for dessert.*

*Maple Meringue Orange Cups (page 65)—a simple microwave dessert that seals in the sweet flavor of oranges with a light maple-flavored meringue.*

*For a quick dessert from the microwave, try individual Lemon Pudding Cakes (page 59).*

*Tropical Starfruit Sippers (page 72) are garnished with slices of starfruit.*

# CONDIMENTS

## CARROT-MANGO RELISH

2 medium carrots, scraped and cut into ⅛-inch slices
¼ cup finely chopped onion
¼ cup unsweetened apple juice
¼ teaspoon ground cardamom
¼ teaspoon dry mustard
⅛ teaspoon ground red pepper
1 cup coarsely chopped mango
2 tablespoons raisins
1 tablespoon grated orange rind

Combine first 6 ingredients in a 1½-quart casserole. Cover with heavy-duty plastic wrap, and microwave at HIGH for 5 to 6 minutes. Add mango, raisins, and orange rind, stirring well. Cover and microwave at HIGH for 2 to 3 minutes or until carrots are tender. Let cool. Yield: 1½ cups (12 calories per tablespoon).

PROTEIN 0.2 / FAT 0.1 / CARBOHYDRATE 3.2 / CHOLESTEROL 0 / IRON 0.1 / SODIUM 2 / CALCIUM 4

# SNAPPY CUCUMBER PICKLES

4 small cucumbers (½ pound)
¼ cup cider vinegar
2 tablespoons water
2 teaspoons sugar
⅛ teaspoon red pepper

Wash cucumbers, and pat dry. Cut each cucumber lengthwise into 4 spears. Place spears, cut side down, in a shallow container; set aside.

Combine vinegar, water, sugar, and pepper in a 1-cup glass measure; stir well. Microwave, uncovered, at HIGH 2 to 3 minutes or until mixture boils. Pour over reserved cucumber spears. Cover and refrigerate at least 8 hours. Serve, using a slotted spoon. Yield: 4 servings (18 calories per serving).

PROTEIN 0.3 / FAT 0.1 / CARBOHYDRATE 4.6 / CHOLESTEROL 0 / IRON 0.3 / SODIUM 1 / CALCIUM 9

# GLAZED APPLES

⅓ cup unsweetened orange juice
1 teaspoon cornstarch
¼ teaspoon ground allspice
2 medium cooking apples, cored and sliced

Combine orange juice, cornstarch, and allspice in a 2-quart casserole, stirring until smooth. Stir in apples. Cover with a glass lid or heavy-duty plastic wrap. Microwave at HIGH for 5 to 6 minutes or until thickened and apples are tender, stirring once. Serve warm. Yield: 4 servings (46 calories per serving).

PROTEIN 0.3 / FAT 0.4 / CARBOHYDRATES 11.4 / FIBER 1.5 / CHOLESTEROL 0 / SODIUM 1 / POTASSIUM 106

# DESSERTS

## DOUBLE STRAWBERRY DELIGHT

4 cups fresh strawberries, hulled and divided
½ cup low-sugar strawberry spread
2 teaspoons cornstarch
2 tablespoons unsweetened orange juice
1 tablespoon grated orange rind
2 tablespoons sliced natural almonds, toasted

Place 1 cup strawberries in container of an electric blender; top with cover, and process until smooth. Combine puree and strawberry spread in a 1-quart baking dish. Microwave, uncovered, at HIGH for 2 to 3 minutes or until mixture begins to boil. Combine cornstarch and orange juice, stirring until smooth. Stir orange juice mixture into strawberry mixture. Microwave, uncovered, at HIGH for 2 minutes or until thickened; stir in orange rind. Cover and chill.

Place remaining 3 cups strawberries in a large bowl. Pour strawberry sauce over berries, tossing gently. To serve, spoon mixture evenly into individual dessert dishes. Sprinkle roasted almonds evenly over each serving. Serve immediately. Yield: 6 servings (65 calories per serving).

PROTEIN 1.1 / FAT 1.6 / CARBOHYDRATE 13.0 / CHOLESTEROL 0 / IRON 0.5 / SODIUM 1 / CALCIUM 22

# RASPBERRY CHIFFON PIE

2 tablespoons reduced-calorie margarine
1 cup crushed vanilla wafers
2 cups fresh raspberries
⅓ cup sugar
⅓ cup skim milk
2 egg yolks
1 envelope unflavored gelatin
½ teaspoon vanilla extract
¼ teaspoon salt
2 egg whites
¼ teaspoon cream of tartar
2 tablespoons sugar
Fresh raspberries (optional)
Fresh mint sprigs (optional)

Place margarine in a 9-inch pie plate. Microwave, uncovered, at HIGH for 30 seconds or until melted. Add crushed wafers, stirring well. Press mixture evenly over bottom and up sides of pie plate. Microwave, uncovered, at HIGH for 1 to 2 minutes or until firm, rotating pie plate a half-turn every 30 seconds. Set aside, let cool.

Place raspberries in container of an electric blender; process until smooth. Strain puree, discarding seeds. Combine puree, sugar, and next 5 ingredients in a 1½-quart baking dish. Microwave, uncovered, at MEDIUM (50% power) 4 to 6 minutes or until mixture boils, stirring every 2 minutes. Let stand 30 to 40 minutes or until mixture thickens slightly.

Beat egg whites (at room temperature) and cream of tartar at high speed of an electric mixer just until foamy. Gradually add 2 tablespoons sugar, 1 tablespoon at a time, beating until stiff peaks form and sugar dissolves (2 to 4 minutes). Gently fold raspberry mixture into meringue. Pour mixture into crust. Chill 2 hours or until firm. If desired, garnish with fresh raspberries and mint sprigs. Yield: 8 servings (168 calories per serving).

PROTEIN 3.6 / FAT 6.5 / CARBOHYDRATE 24.4 / CHOLESTEROL 68 / IRON 0.7 / SODIUM 185 / CALCIUM 33

# MARINATED PINEAPPLE WEDGES

¼ cup water
¼ cup unsweetened frozen apple juice concentrate,
  thawed and undiluted
1 tablespoon freshly squeezed lime juice
½ teaspoon grated lime rind
¼ teaspoon ground allspice
1 tablespoon Triple Sec or other orange-flavored liqueur
1 small fresh pineapple

Combine first 5 ingredients in a 2-cup glass measure. Microwave, uncovered, at HIGH for 2½ to 3 minutes or until boiling. Let mixture cool slightly. Stir in liqueur, and set aside.

Peel and trim eyes from pineapple, removing core and reserving leaves. Cut pineapple lengthwise into four 3-ounce wedges. Place wedges in a shallow container. Reserve remaining pineapple for other uses. Pour reserved liqueur mixture over pineapple wedges. Cover and marinate in refrigerator 4 hours or overnight, turning wedges occasionally. Drain wedges, discarding marinade. Garnish with pineapple leaves. Yield: 4 servings (84 calories per serving).

PROTEIN 0.4 / FAT 0.5 / CARBOHYDRATE 19.3 / CHOLESTEROL 0 / IRON 0.5 / SODIUM 5 /
CALCIUM 11

# PEACHES 'N' CREAM

1 cup vanilla ice milk, softened
½ teaspoon ground cinnamon
1 tablespoon plus 1½ teaspoons brown sugar
1 tablespoon plus 1½ teaspoons cornstarch
½ teaspoon ground cinnamon
¼ teaspoon ground ginger
1 tablespoon lemon juice
½ teaspoon almond extract
3 cups peeled, sliced peaches
Vegetable cooking spray
Fresh mint sprigs (optional)

Combine ice milk and ½ teaspoon cinnamon, stirring well. Cover and freeze until firm.

Combine brown sugar and next 5 ingredients in a large bowl. Add peaches and toss gently. Spoon into an 8-inch square baking dish that has been coated with cooking spray. Cover with wax paper and microwave at HIGH for 6 to 8 minutes or until peaches are tender, giving dish a half-turn after 4 minutes. Let stand 2 minutes. Spoon ½ cup peach mixture into individual dessert dishes. Top each serving with ¼ cup ice milk. Garnish with fresh mint sprigs, if desired. Yield: 4 servings (129 calories per serving).

PROTEIN 2.2 / FAT 1.7 / CARBOHYDRATE 28.2 / CHOLESTEROL 5 / IRON 0.5 / SODIUM 27 / CALCIUM 61

# LEMON PUDDING CAKES

¼ cup plus 2 tablespoons sugar
⅓ cup all-purpose flour
¼ teaspoon salt
2 eggs, separated
¾ cup skim milk
2 tablespoons lemon juice
1 tablespoon grated lemon rind
Vegetable cooking spray
Fresh blueberries (optional)
Lemon slices (optional)
Fresh mint sprigs (optional)

Combine first 3 ingredients in a medium bowl; set aside.

Beat egg yolks at high speed of an electric mixer until thick and lemon colored; add skim milk and lemon juice, beating well. Add egg mixture to dry ingredients; beat well. Beat egg whites (at room temperature) at high speed of an electric mixer until soft peaks form. Gently fold egg whites and lemon rind into milk mixture.

Pour batter evenly into 6 (6-ounce) custard cups that have been coated with cooking spray. Place 3 custard cups in microwave oven. Microwave, uncovered, at MEDIUM-HIGH (70% power) for 2 to 2½ minutes, rotating a half-turn after 1 minute. Let stand 2 minutes. Repeat procedure with remaining custard cups. If desired, garnish with blueberries, lemon slices, and fresh mint sprigs. Serve warm. Yield: 6 servings (116 calories per serving).

PROTEIN 3.9 / FAT 2.2 / CARBOHYDRATE 20.5 / CHOLESTEROL 92 / IRON 0.6 / SODIUM 137 / CALCIUM 51

# TROPICAL TRIFLE

¼ cup sugar
¼ teaspoon salt
3 tablespoons cornstarch
1¾ cups plus 2 tablespoons skim milk
1 egg yolk
2 tablespoons cream sherry
1 (8-ounce) can unsweetened pineapple chunks, drained
1 kiwi, peeled and sliced
½ cup fresh strawberries, sliced
1 medium mango, peeled, seeded, and cubed
4 (1-ounce) slices angel food cake, cut into ½-inch cubes
1 starfruit, sliced and seeded
Strawberry fan (optional)
Fresh mint sprigs (optional)

Combine sugar, salt, and cornstarch in a 1½-quart casserole. Gradually add skim milk, stirring with a wire whisk. Microwave, uncovered, at MEDIUM-HIGH (70% power) for 5 to 6 minutes or until thickened, stirring every 2 minutes.

Combine egg yolk and sherry, beating with a wire whisk. Gradually stir about one fourth of hot mixture into egg mixture; add to remaining hot mixture, stirring constantly. Microwave, uncovered, at MEDIUM-HIGH for 1 minute. Cover with plastic wrap, gently pressing directly on pudding. Chill until thickened.

Combine pineapple, kiwi, strawberries, and mango. Line bottom of a 2-quart glass bowl with half of fruit. Cover fruit with angel food cake. Spread half of chilled pudding over cake. Spoon remaining half of fruit over pudding. Cover with remaining pudding. Top with starfruit. Chill thoroughly. If desired, garnish with strawberry fan and fresh mint sprigs. Yield: 6 servings (197 calories per serving).

PROTEIN 4.7 / FAT 1.4 / CARBOHYDRATE 42.7 / CHOLESTEROL 47 / IRON 0.5 / SODIUM 168 / CALCIUM 131

# EASY STRAWBERRY SUNDAES

½ cup plus 2 tablespoons low-sugar strawberry spread
2 tablespoons unsweetened orange juice
3 cups vanilla ice milk
2 medium bananas, sliced

Combine strawberry spread and orange juice in a 2-cup glass measure; cover with wax paper. Microwave at MEDIUM (50% power) for 2 to 3 minutes or until mixture is thoroughly heated, stirring once.

Scoop ½ cup ice milk into 6 dessert dishes; top evenly with banana slices. Spoon 2 tablespoons warm strawberry mixture over each serving. Serve immediately. Yield: 6 servings (151 calories per serving).

PROTEIN 3.0 / FAT 3.0 / CARBOHYDRATE 29.3 / CHOLESTEROL 9 / IRON 0.2 / SODIUM 53 / CALCIUM 91

# RUM-PINEAPPLE BOAT

1 tablespoon unsweetened grated coconut
1 large fresh pineapple
3 tablespoons dark rum
2 tablespoons brown sugar

Place coconut in a custard cup; microwave at HIGH for 3 to 4 minutes or until toasted, stirring after every minute. Set aside.

Cut a slice from side of pineapple, leaving top intact to form a boat. Scoop out pulp, leaving ¼- to ½-inch-thick shell; set aside. Discard slice. Cut pineapple pulp into bite-size pieces, discarding core. Combine pulp, rum, and brown sugar in a medium bowl; stir well. Cover with heavy-duty plastic wrap and microwave at HIGH for 4 to 5 minutes or until thoroughly heated. Spoon pineapple mixture into reserved shell. Sprinkle with toasted coconut. Serve warm. Yield: 6 servings (98 calories per ½-cup serving).

PROTEIN 0.5 / FAT 1.0 / CARBOHYDRATE 19.3 / CHOLESTEROL 0 / IRON 0.6 / SODIUM 3 / CALCIUM 12

# COCONUT CUSTARD

1 cup skim milk
2 tablespoons sugar
2 tablespoons cornstarch
1 tablespoon margarine
2 eggs, separated
1 cup unsweetened pineapple juice
1 tablespoon lime juice
¼ teaspoon rum extract
2 tablespoons powdered sugar
½ teaspoon coconut extract
2 tablespoons plus 2 teaspoons unsweetened grated
    coconut, toasted

Combine skim milk, sugar, cornstarch, and margarine in a 1-quart glass measure. Microwave, uncovered, at HIGH for 2 to 3 minutes or until mixture begins to boil, stirring once. Combine egg yolks and pineapple juice in a medium bowl; beat well with a wire whisk. Gradually stir about one fourth of hot milk mixture into egg mixture; add to remaining milk mixture, stirring constantly. Microwave, uncovered, at HIGH for 3 to 5 minutes or until thickened, stirring after every minute. Remove from oven; stir in lime juice and rum extract.

Spoon mixture evenly into four 6-ounce custard cups. Beat egg whites (at room temperature) at high speed of an electric mixer 1 minute. Gradually add sugar, 1 tablespoon at a time, beating until stiff peaks form and sugar dissolves (2 to 4 minutes). Gently fold in coconut extract. Spread meringue mixture evenly over custard. Microwave, uncovered, at HIGH for 1 to 1½ minutes or until meringue is set. Sprinkle 2 teaspoons coconut over each serving. Serve immediately. Yield: 4 servings (200 calories per serving).

PROTEIN 5.6 / FAT 8.0 / CARBOHYDRATE 26.5 / CHOLESTEROL 138 / IRON 0.8 / SODIUM 102 / CALCIUM 102

# HONEY-APPLE CRISP

6 medium cooking apples, peeled, cored, and thinly sliced
¼ cup honey
2 tablespoons golden raisins
2 teaspoons grated orange rind
½ cup all-purpose flour
⅓ cup quick-cooking oats, uncooked
3 tablespoons brown sugar
½ teaspoon ground allspice
3 tablespoons reduced-calorie margarine

Combine apple slices, honey, raisins, and orange rind in a medium bowl; toss gently. Place apple mixture in an 8-inch square baking dish; set aside.

Combine flour, oats, brown sugar, and allspice in a small bowl; cut in margarine with a pastry blender until mixture resembles coarse meal. Spoon flour mixture evenly over apple mixture. Cover with heavy-duty plastic wrap, and microwave at HIGH for 8 to 10 minutes. Let stand 10 minutes. To serve, spoon crisp evenly into individual dessert dishes. Yield: 8 servings (200 calories per serving).

PROTEIN 2.2 / FAT 3.7 / CARBOHYDRATE 42.4 / CHOLESTEROL 0 / IRON 0.9 / SODIUM 44 / CALCIUM 16

# MAPLE MERINGUE ORANGE CUPS

2 medium-size navel oranges
2 tablespoons reduced-calorie maple syrup, divided
2 egg whites
⅛ teaspoon cream of tartar
⅛ teaspoon ground nutmeg
Orange rind strips

Cut oranges in half crosswise. Clip membranes, and remove pulp, being careful not to puncture bottom. Coarsely chop pulp; mix with 1 tablespoon maple syrup. Spoon pulp mixture into orange cups. Place in a microwave-safe 8-inch cake dish. Microwave, uncovered, at HIGH for 2 to 2½ minutes.

Beat egg whites (at room temperature) and cream of tartar until foamy. Gradually add remaining syrup, beating until stiff peaks form. Spread meringue over top of each shell; seal edges. Microwave, uncovered, at HIGH for 1 to 1½ minutes or until meringue is set. Sprinkle with nutmeg. Garnish with orange rind strips. Yield: 4 servings (44 calories per serving).

PROTEIN 2.4 / FAT 0.1 / CARBOHYDRATE 9.4 / CHOLESTEROL 0 / IRON 0.1 / SODIUM 34 / CALCIUM 30

# BERRY DUO IN WINE

¼ cup Chablis or other dry white wine
3 tablespoons sugar
1 tablespoon lemon juice
½ teaspoon grated lemon rind
1 pint fresh strawberries, washed, hulled, and halved
½ cup fresh or frozen blueberries, thawed
1 tablespoon Triple Sec or other orange-flavored liqueur

Combine wine and sugar in a 1-quart casserole. Microwave, uncovered, at HIGH for 2½ to 3 minutes or until sugar dissolves. Stir in lemon juice, lemon rind, strawberries, and blueberries. Microwave, uncovered, at HIGH for 1 to 2 minutes. Sprinkle fruit mixture with liqueur. Cover and chill thoroughly. Spoon chilled fruit mixture into 4 individual dessert dishes. Yield: 4 servings (84 calories per serving).

PROTEIN 0.6 / FAT 0.4 / CARBOHYDRATE 19.1 / CHOLESTEROL 0 / IRON 0.4 / SODIUM 3 / CALCIUM 13

# GLAZED BANANAS

1 tablespoon margarine
1 tablespoon firmly packed brown sugar
⅛ teaspoon ground cinnamon
⅛ teaspoon ground ginger
⅛ teaspoon ground nutmeg
⅓ cup unsweetened orange juice
2 medium bananas, split lengthwise and halved
2 tablespoons chopped unsalted peanuts

Place margarine in a 2-quart casserole. Microwave at HIGH for 30 seconds or until margarine melts. Add brown sugar, cinnamon, ginger, nutmeg, and orange juice; mix well. Microwave at HIGH for 5½ to 6 minutes, stirring after 3 minutes. Add bananas, turning to coat well. Microwave at HIGH for 1 minute or until thoroughly heated. Sprinkle with peanuts. Serve immediately. Yield: 4 servings (129 calories per serving).

PROTEIN 2.0 / FAT 5.4 / CARBOHYDRATE 20.5 / CHOLESTEROL 0 / IRON 0.4 / SODIUM 36 / CALCIUM 14

# BANANAS FOSTER OVER ICE MILK

¼ cup unsweetened apple juice
1 tablespoon lemon juice
⅛ teaspoon ground cinnamon
1 medium banana, split lengthwise and halved
2 tablespoons light rum
1 cup vanilla ice milk

Combine apple juice, lemon juice, and cinnamon in a 1-quart casserole, stirring well. Add banana, turning to coat well. Cover with plastic wrap and microwave at HIGH for 1½ to 2 minutes or until thoroughly heated; set aside, and keep warm.

Place rum in a 1-cup glass measure, and microwave at HIGH for 15 to 30 seconds or until heated. (Do not boil.) Pour over banana, and ignite with a long match; baste banana with juice mixture until flames die. Serve immediately over ½-cup portions of ice milk. Yield: 2 servings (163 calories per serving).

PROTEIN 3.2 / FAT 3.1 / CARBOHYDRATE 32.8 / FIBER 0.9 / CHOLESTEROL 9 / SODIUM 54 / POTASSIUM 415

# DRESSED-UP PEARS

1 cup halved fresh strawberries
2 tablespoons water
2 teaspoons cornstarch
1 tablespoon Triple Sec or other orange-flavored liqueur
8 canned unsweetened pear halves, chilled
Zest of 1 orange

Place strawberries in container of an electric blender; process until pureed. Transfer strawberries to a small bowl, and set aside. Combine water and cornstarch in a small bowl, stirring until blended. Add cornstarch mixture and Triple Sec to strawberries;

stir until well blended. Cover with heavy-duty plastic wrap, and microwave at HIGH for 4 to 5 minutes or until sauce thickens and boils. Chill thoroughly.

Divide sauce among 4 individual dessert plates with slightly raised edges; place two pear halves on top of sauce in each plate. Garnish with orange zest before serving. Yield: 4 servings (128 calories per serving).

PROTEIN 0.9 / FAT 0.8 / CARBOHYDRATE 30.3 / FIBER 4.8 / CHOLESTEROL 0 / SODIUM 0 / POTASSIUM 268

# PINEAPPLE DESSERT SAUCE OVER ICE MILK

1 (20-ounce) can unsweetened crushed pineapple, undrained
1 teaspoon cornstarch
1 tablespoon Grand Marnier or other orange-flavored liqueur
2 tablespoons flaked coconut
¼ teaspoon grated orange rind
1 quart vanilla ice milk

Drain pineapple, reserving ¼ cup juice in a 1-quart glass measure. Set pineapple aside.

Add cornstarch to reserved juice, stirring until well blended. Stir in pineapple and liqueur. Microwave at HIGH for 1 to 2 minutes; stir well, and microwave at HIGH for 3 to 4 minutes or until thickened. Stir in coconut and orange rind; to serve, spoon ¼-cup portions of warm pineapple sauce over ½-cup portions of ice milk. Yield: 8 servings (133 calories per serving).

PROTEIN 2.8 / FAT 3.6 / CARBOHYDRATE 22.6 / FIBER 0.7 / CHOLESTEROL 9 / SODIUM 57 / POTASSIUM 199

# MICROWAVE VANILLA CUSTARD

2 cups skim milk
4 tablespoons sugar, divided
1 egg, beaten
1 tablespoon plus 1 teaspoon cornstarch
½ teaspoon vanilla extract
4 fresh strawberries

Combine skim milk and 3 tablespoons sugar in a 2-quart glass measure. Microwave at HIGH for 5 to 6 minutes or just until mixture begins to boil, stirring at 3 minute intervals.

Combine egg and remaining 1 tablespoon sugar in a small bowl; beat well, using a wire whisk. Gradually add cornstarch, beating constantly. Gradually stir one fourth of hot milk mixture into egg mixture; add to remaining milk mixture, stirring constantly. Microwave at HIGH for 2 to 3 minutes or until thickened, stirring every 30 seconds. Remove from microwave, and stir 3 minutes. Stir in vanilla.

Spoon mixture into 4 dessert dishes; chill until set. Garnish each with a strawberry. Yield: 4 servings (128 calories per serving).

PROTEIN 5.8 / FAT 1.7 / CARBOHYDRATES 22.2 / FIBER 0.3 / CHOLESTEROL 81 / SODIUM 81 / POTASSIUM 243

# MICROWAVE PEAR CRUNCH

2 teaspoons slivered almonds
3 medium-size ripe pears, chopped
2 teaspoons lemon juice
¼ teaspoon almond extract
1 tablespoon all-purpose flour
1 tablespoon firmly packed dark brown sugar
1 tablespoon margarine
2 tablespoons regular oats, uncooked

Place almonds in a custard cup. Cover with heavy-duty plastic wrap, and microwave at HIGH for 1 to 1½ minutes or until almonds are toasted; set aside.

Combine pears, lemon juice, and almond extract in a medium bowl, tossing well. Divide among 4 (6-ounce) custard cups or individual baking dishes; set aside.

Combine flour and brown sugar; cut in margarine with a pastry blender until mixture resembles coarse meal. Stir in oats and reserved almonds. Divide among reserved custard cups.

Microwave at HIGH for 6 minutes or until pears are tender, rotating cups after 3 minutes. Yield: 4 servings (139 calories per serving).

PROTEIN 1.4 / FAT 4.3 / CARBOHYDRATE 25.9 / FIBER 3.5 / CHOLESTEROL 0 / SODIUM 36 / POTASSIUM 192

# BEVERAGES

## STARFRUIT SIPPERS

2 tablespoons sugar
2 tablespoons water
1 tablespoon chopped crystallized ginger
2 medium starfruit (6½ ounces), sliced and seeded
1 cup sliced fresh strawberries
Sugar
2 cups Chablis or other dry white wine, chilled
¾ cup sodium-free seltzer water, chilled
Starfruit slices (optional)

Combine 2 tablespoons sugar, water, and ginger in a 1-cup glass measure. Microwave, uncovered, at HIGH for 2 to 3 minutes or until mixture forms a light syrup, stirring after every minute. Cool slightly. Place starfruit, strawberries, and sugar mixture in container of an electric blender; process until smooth. Cover and chill thoroughly.

To serve, lightly moisten the rims of four 10-ounce glasses. Place sugar in a saucer; spin rim of each glass in sugar. Combine fruit mixture and wine, stirring well. Pour evenly into glasses. Add 3 tablespoons seltzer water to each glass; stir gently. Garnish with starfruit slices, if desired. Serve immediately. Yield: 4 servings (93 calories per 1-cup serving).

PROTEIN 0.6 / FAT 0.3 / CARBOHYDRATE 23.2 / CHOLESTEROL 0 / IRON 1.5 / SODIUM 19 / CALCIUM 28

# PINEAPPLE-MINT COOLERS

1 (6-ounce) can frozen lemonade concentrate, thawed and
   diluted
2 tablespoons fresh mint leaves
2 cups unsweetened pineapple juice
1 (6½-ounce) bottle sparkling mineral water, chilled
Ice cubes
Fresh mint sprigs (optional)

Combine 1 cup prepared lemonade and mint leaves in a 4-cup glass
measure. Reserve remaining lemonade for other uses. Microwave
lemonade mixture, uncovered, at HIGH 2 to 3 minutes or until
thoroughly heated. Let stand 5 minutes. Stir in pineapple juice.
Cover and chill at least 2 hours; strain. Lightly stir in sparkling
mineral water. Serve over ice. Garnish with fresh mint sprigs, if
desired. Yield: 4 cups (94 calories per 1-cup serving).

PROTEIN 0.5 / FAT 0.1 / CARBOHYDRATE 23.6 / CHOLESTEROL 0 / IRON 0.5 / SODIUM 14 /
CALCIUM 25

# CINNAMON HOT CHOCOLATE

2 tablespoons sugar
3 tablespoons Dutch process cocoa
2 tablespoons instant coffee powder
½ teaspoon ground cinnamon
4 cups skim milk
4 (3-inch) sticks cinnamon

Combine sugar, cocoa, coffee powder, ground cinnamon, and skim milk in a large bowl, stirring well. Cover with heavy-duty plastic wrap and microwave at HIGH for 6 to 8 minutes or until thoroughly heated, stirring after 4 minutes. Ladle chocolate into mugs; add 1 stick cinnamon to each, and serve immediately. Yield: 4 cups (130 calories per 1-cup serving).

PROTEIN 9.4 / FAT 1.5 / CARBOHYDRATE 22.2 / FIBER 0.8 / CHOLESTEROL 5 / SODIUM 158 / POTASSIUM 502

# INDEX

Apple(s)
glazed, 54
honey crisp, 64
Asparagus
salad with watercress dressing, 4–5
-yellow squash salad, 10
Aspic, tomato-vegetable, 12

Bananas
Foster over ice milk, 68
glazed, 67
Barbecued chicken, 28
Beans
three-bean salad, hot, 6
Beef
burritos, -zucchini, 22–23
sloppy joes, 31
-vegetable soup, quick, 3
Berry duo in wine, 66
Beverages
hot chocolate, cinnamon, 74
pineapple-mint coolers, 73
starfruit sippers, 72
Brie dressing, warm, 5
Brown rice with pecans, 41–42
Burritos, zucchini-beef, 22–23

Cake, lemon pudding, 59
Candied sweet potatoes, 48
Carrot(s)
baby, lemony, 47
-mango-relish, 53
and peas, minted, 47
Catfish, southern pecan, 29
Celery and corn mingle, 46
Cheese
Brie dressing, warm, 5
chicken mozzarella, 21
pita salad sandwiches, cheesy, 39

Chicken
barbecued, 28
with creamy gravy, country, 25–26
cutlets, prize, 17
and dumplings, 19
mozzarella, 21
salad, shredded, 36
stew, safari, 33
teriyaki, 30
Chile
green chile soup, creamy, 2
Chocolate
hot chocolate, cinnamon, 74
Cilantro-seasoned corn, 45
Cinnamon hot chocolate, 74
Citrus dressing, 14
Coconut custard, 63
Condiments
apples, glazed, 54
pickles, snappy cucumber, 54
relish, carrot-mango, 53
Corn
and celery mingle, 46
cilantro-seasoned, 45
and okra, garden, 49
on the cob, herbed, 50
Cornish hens, stuffed, 23–24
Couscous with parsley, 42
Creamy
green chile soup, 2
gravy, 26
Creole eggs, 15–16
Curry(ied)
lamb and vegetable medley, 16–17
rice, 44
Custard
coconut, 63
vanilla microwave, 70
Cutlets, chicken prize, 17

Desserts
  bananas, glazed, 67
  bananas Foster over ice milk, 68
  berry duo in wine, 66
  crisp, honey-apple, 64
  custard
    coconut, 63
    vanilla microwave, 70
  orange cups, maple meringue, 65
  peaches 'n' cream, 58
  pear crunch, microwave, 71
  pears, dressed-up, 68–69
  pie, raspberry chiffon, 56
  pineapple wedges, marinated, 57
  pudding cakes, lemon, 59
  rum-pineapple boat, 62
  sauce, pineapple over ice milk, 69
  strawberry delight, double, 55
  sundaes, easy strawberry, 61
  trifle, tropical, 60
Dilled new potato halves, 50
Dumplings and chicken, 19

Eggs, creole, 15–16

Fish
  catfish, southern pecan, 29
  flounder, lemon, 32
  salmon loaf, continental, 37
  sole en papillote with garden vegetables,
    34
  See also Seafood
Flounder, lemon, 32
Fruit
  salad with citrus dressing, 14
  See also specific name
Fruit desserts
  apple-honey crisp, 64
  bananas, glazed, 67
  bananas Foster over ice milk, 68
  berry duo in wine, 66
  orange cups, maple meringue, 65
  peaches 'n' cream, 58
  pear crunch, 71
  pears, dressed-up, 68–69
  pineapple dessert sauce over ice milk, 69
  pineapple-rum boat, 62
  pineapple wedges, marinated, 57
  raspberry chiffon pie, 56
  strawberry delight, double, 55
  tropical trifle, 60

Ginger-sesame rice, 43
Glazed
  apples, 54
  bananas, 67

Gravy, creamy, 26
Green salad with warm Brie dressing, 5
Grits and ham pie, 27

Ham and grits pie, 27
Herb(ed)
  cilantro-seasoned corn, 45
  corn on the cob, 50
  dilled new potato halves, 50
  minted peas and carrots, 47
  mint-pineapple coolers, 73
  -parsley rice, 43–44
  parsley with couscous, 42
  rosemary grilled lamb chops, 20
  tomato bouillon, 1
Honey-apple crisp, 64
Hot chocolate, cinnamon, 74

Ice milk
  bananas Foster over, 68
  pineapple dessert sauce over, 69
  strawberry sundaes, easy, 61
Lamb
  chops, rosemary grilled, 20
  shish kabobs, 38
  and vegetable medley, curried, 16–17
Lemon
  carrots, baby, 47
  flounder, 32
  pudding cakes, 59
Lettuce
  green salad with warm Brie dressing, 13
  wilted salad, 13
Loaf, salmon continental, 37

Mango-carrot relish, 53
Maple meringue orange cups, 65
Marinated pineapple wedges, 57
Meat. See Beef; Lamb; Pork
Meringue, maple orange cups, 65
Mexicali tacos, 24–25
Mexican rice, 41
Mint(ed)
  peas and carrots, 47
  -pineapple coolers, 73
Mozzarella, chicken, 21

Nuts
  pecan catfish, southern, 29
  pecans with brown rice, 41–42

Okra and corn, garden, 49
Orange cups, maple meringue, 65

Parsley
  with couscous, 42

-herbed rice, 43–44
Peaches 'n' cream, 58
Pear(s)
    crunch, microwave, 71
    dressed-up, 68–69
Peas and carrots, minted, 47
Pecan(s)
    with brown rice, 41–42
    catfish, southern, 29
Pepper(s)
    green chile soup, creamy, 2
    salad, sweet, 8
Pickles, snappy cucumber, 54
Pie
    ham and grits, 27
    raspberry chiffon, 56
Pineapple
    dessert sauce over ice milk, 69
    -mint coolers, 73
    -rum boat, 62
    salad with poppy seed dressing, 7
    wedges, marinated, 57
Pita salad sandwiches, cheesy, 39
Poppy seed dressing, 7
    -yogurt, 8–9
Pork
    ham and grits pie, 27
Potato, halves new dilled, 50
Poultry. See Chicken; Cornish hens; Turkey
Pudding cakes, lemon, 59

Raspberry chiffon pie, 56
Relish, carrot-mango, 53
Rice
    brown, with pecans, 41–42
    curried, 44
    herbed-parsley, 43–44
    Mexican, 41
    savory, 40
    sesame-ginger, 43
Rosemary grilled lamb chops, 20
Rum-pineapple boat, 62

Salad
    asparagus with watercress dressing, 4–5
    asparagus–yellow squash, 10
    aspic, tomato-vegetable, 12
    chicken, shredded, 36
    fruit with citrus dressing, 14
    green with warm Brie dressing, 5
    pepper, sweet, 8
    pineapple with poppy seed dressing, 7
    pita sandwiches, cheesy, 39
    spinach with yogurt–poppy seed dress-
        ing, 8–9
    sweet potato, 11

three-bean, hot, 6
tomato
    cherry, 9
    -vegetable aspic, 12
wilted lettuce, 13
Salad dressing
    Brie, warm, 5
    citrus, 14
    poppy seed, 7
    watercress, 4–5
    yogurt–poppy seed, 8–9
Salmon loaf, continental, 37
Sandwiches
    pita salad, cheesy, 39
    sloppy joes, 31
    turkey joes, 18
Sauce
    dessert, pineapple, 69
    gravy, creamy, 26
    spinach, 51
Seafood
    shrimp in oyster sauce, 35
Sesame-ginger rice, 43
Shish kabobs, 38
Shrimp in oyster sauce, 35
Sloppy joes, 31
Sole en papillote with garden vegetables, 34
Soup
    green chile, creamy, 2
    tomato bouillon, herbed, 1
    vegetable-beef, quick, 3
Spaghetti squash with summer vegetables,
    52
Spinach
    salad with yogurt–poppy seed dressing,
        8–9
    sauce with fresh tomatoes, 51
Squash
    spaghetti squash with summer vegeta-
        bles, 52
    yellow squash–asparagus salad, 10
Starfruit sippers, 72
Stew, chicken safari, 33
Strawberry
    delight, double, 55
    sundaes, easy, 61
Stuffed Cornish hens, 23–24
Sundaes, easy strawberry, 61
Sweet potato(es)
    candied, 48
    salad, 11

Tacos, Mexicali, 24–25
Tomato(es)
    aspic, vegetable, 12
    bouillon, herbed, 1

cherry tomato salad, 9
  fresh, with spinach sauce, 51
Trifle, tropical, 60
Turkey
  joes, 18
  tacos, Mexicali, 24–25

Vanilla custard, microwave, 70
Vegetable(s)
  -beef soup, quick, 3
  and lamb medley, curried, 16–17

with sole en papillote, 34
with spaghetti squash, summer, 52
-tomato aspic, 12
*See also specific name*

Watercress dressing, 4–5
Wilted lettuce salad, 13

Yogurt–poppy seed dressing, 8–9

Zucchini-beef burritos, 22–23